Where to Buy "Container Gardens for Butterflies":

The book is available through amazon.com, plus many garden centers and book sellers. To locate your nearest source or place an order with the publisher, contact us at:

Pamela Crawford & Associates, 12278 Big Canoe, 98 Robins Nest, Jasper, GA 30143
Phone: 561-371-2719 Web site: www.pamela-crawford.com
Email: info@pamela-crawford.com

Credits:

Author: Pamela Crawford
Marketing Director: Barbara Hadsell
Cover Design and Graphic Design Assistance: Elaine Weber Designs, Inc. (www.ewdlogos.com)
Proofreader: Barbara Iderosa, Best Editing Service, Pahokee, Florida

Photography: All photos by Pamela Crawford except for the following: Through Shutterstock: p.3, Butterflies, Georgi Baird. p. 7, top center, Jim Nelson. p. 32, Kate Scott; p. 33. Lisa Basile Ellwood. p. 38, Cathy Keifer. buckeye, p. 39, Jody Wiele, monarch, p. 39. Danita Delmont; painted lady, p. 39, Maia Kennedy; spicebush swallowtail, p. 39. David Trevarthen; viceroy, p. 39. Jim Nelson; dill, p. 40. Carroteater; fennel, p. 40, Richard Peterson. swallowtail caterpillar, top right, p. 40, Mabeline72. swallowtail caterpillar, middle, p. 40 Sari Oneal, swallowtail photo, bottom, Agosto. Purple butterfly weed, p. 41 Susan Hodgson. passionflower, p. 41, Watin, p. 46, hummingbird, Holly Miller-Pollack. morning cloak, p. 74, Danita Delmont. buckeye, p. 72, buckeye, p. 72, Jody Wiele. painted lady, p. 72, Maia Kennedy. monarch, p. 114, Melody Mellinger. monarch, top center, Nikola Bilic.

Proven Winners: Hydrangea and butterfly bush, p. 36, monarchs, top left & right, p. 116. butterfly bushes, coneflower, and hydrangea, p. 118. viburnum, p. 132. spirea, poker plant, rose, echinacea, p. 126. hibiscus, salvias, p. 130.

Southern Living Plants, Plant Development Services: lobelia, loropetalum, p. 122, 130. ilex, 122, 126, 130. rose, p. 130

Suntory: Vinca, p. 133. Scaevola, p. 80-81. torenia, 80 & 88. vinca, 165

Misc. photo sources: black swallowtail, p. 39, gulf fritillary, p. 39, Harvey Cotten; *Asclepias curassavica*, p. 38, container garden, p. 59, Paul Sayegh.

Photos by David Akoubian, Bear Woods Photography: p. 69, 71, 73, 82, 119, 120-121, 123 (tall photo), p. 127-129, 131, 132, 134, 135,

Published by Pamela Crawford & Associates, Jasper, GA, 2023.
Printed in South Korea.

ISBN 13: 978-0-9829971-5-4
ISBN 10: 0-9829971-5-9

Contents

Thank You

Barbara Hadsell, Marketing Director, who has worked for years on research, marketing, and presentations for all of our books.

Elaine Weber, the graphic designer, worked enthusiastically with me on some very tight deadlines.

Graham Kinsman and his wife, Michele, who worked with me to develop the side-planted baskets shown throughout the book.

Why I Wrote This Book

I have been fascinated by butterflies since I began gardening. They look like flying flowers to me, adding glorious beauty and movement to my garden.

I'd been hearing about the plight of the butterflies for years. A few years ago, I noticed that I didn't see as many butterflies in my own garden as I used to. I began researching this topic and discovered some alarming facts (from the Xerces Society):

1. Five butterflies have gone extinct in the US since 1950; an additional 29 butterflies are listed as endangered nationwide, and six are listed as threatened.

2. In the early 1990's, nearly 700 million monarchs made the flight annually from the northern plains of the U.S. and Canada to Mexico to overwinter. More than a million of them overwintered on the California coast. Their population declined 85% in just two decades.

3. Monarchs only lay their eggs on one plant species - milkweed. Loss of the milkweed breeding habitat is due to the widespread use of herbicides-resistant crops. New vegetable varieties no longer die when they are sprayed with these weed killers. So, some genius figured out that vegetable fields could be

sprayed from planes with herbicides to kill the weeds without killing the crops. In doing so, the plant killers kill all the wildflowers that surround the fields, including alarming numbers of milkweed plants.

4. The main reasons for butterfly extinction are habitat loss, climate change, disease, pesticides, and invasive plants.

Many garden clubs, government agencies, and conservation societies are working on ways to slow the butterfly decline. Efforts include promoting the use of native plants, sustainable forestry practices, habitat conservation, just to name a few.

Conservation efforts will be ongoing for the forseeable future. In the meantime, I decided to write this book to encourage people to plant simple, easy-to-find, inexpensive, flowering plants in containers on decks and patios. I point out which plants in my containers attract the most butterflies.

The flowers in the containers in this book are largely annuals that are readily-available in local garden centers.

I would prefer recommending strictly native plants for butterfly conservation. I understand the importance of planting native plants in the landscape. However, native plants are not anywhere near as plentiful in local garden centers as annuals are. For example, there are no native plant nurseries within a 45-minute drive of my home. Many people would drive that far for permanent, landscape plants. However, many more would not drive 45 minutes to buy a few plants for a decorative planter. Plus, native plants are often expensive and sold in pot sizes that are too large for most mixed container gardens.

I look forward to a time when native plant growers work closely on a national program with all garden centers (including chain stores) to bring in as many natives in 4" pots as possible, keeping in mind low prices.

In the meantime, we need to do something positive to keep our beautiful butterflies alive! Plant simple, pretty flowers and watch them come!

Left: The white bowl includes hot pink pentas as a centerpiece, surrounded by yellow and pink coleus and blue torenia.

The bright colored containers include red geraniums, blue salvia, and orange gaillardia.

These plantings attracted a lot of butterflies because of the variety of flowers

Chapter 1

Growing Basics

Skim this chapter before planting your first container. It will save you a lot of time, money, and trouble – and make container gardening a lot easier for you.

I have planted tens of thousands of plants in containers in order to find out what's easy and what's not. This chapter tells the story.

See this chapter for easy instructions on these key areas:

- ❖ Seven easy ways to kill plants
- ❖ Differences between container gardens and gardens planted in the ground
- ❖ My plant trials
- ❖ Shopping for plants
- ❖ Plants live longer in large containers.
- ❖ Use centerpieces for mixed plantings.
- ❖ Assessing light conditions
- ❖ Easy planting and maintenance
- ❖ Planting demos
- ❖ Fertilizer
- ❖ Watering basics

Opposite: A butterfly fantasy!
Above: Left to right: Eastern Tiger Swallowtail, Monarch, Red-spotted Purple

Seven Easy Ways to Kill Plants

1. Buy the Wrong Plants

Most beginners buy plants that don't meet their expectations simply because they don't understand plant's' flowering habits - or particular plants are erratic performers.

Take this book with you to your garden center. Check out the plants in the last chapter and you'll have a much better chance of long-lived container gardens.

2. Buy the Wrong Potting Mix

Don't skimp on your potting mix. Good potting mix costs a little bit more but makes all the difference. The plants grow larger and live longer with quality potting mix. Do not buy topsoil, garden soil, or potting soil for containers. It is too heavy, and the plants may rot and die quickly.

Look for a brand name you trust. Peters, Miracle Grow, Lambert's and Fafard (along with many others) offer top-quality potting mixes.

3. Buy the Wrong Fertilizer

I have killed plants by using fertilizers several times. My first lawn died from over fertilization. Years later, an entire garden (my landscaping company planted) died because the popular, slow-release fertilizer we used released all three months' worth of nutrients at once. Water causes the fertilizer to activate, and we had a lot of rain. I don't want to kill plants because of such a routine occurrence! See more about fertilizer on pages 28 - 29.

4. Water Incorrectly

Like people, plants need water to live. However, if you give plants too much, they die from drowning. If you give them too little, they die of thirst.

Luckily, knowing when and how much to water is quite easy. See pages 30 - 31 for complete watering information.

5. Pile Potting Mix Around the Stem of the Plant

If potting mix or organic mulch comes into contact with the stem of many plants, the stem rots, killing the plant. It is quite easy to avoid this plight by simply planting the plants a little higher.

To help retain water, some people like to put organic mulch on top of the potting mix after they have planted a container. This method works fine on large plants, like azaleas or ti plants, provided you don't pile the mulch up around the stem. However, on small annuals, like impatiens, it is quite difficult to mulch without harming the plant.

6. Plant in a Pot Without Holes in the Bottom

If your pots don't have holes in the bottom for drainage, the plants will die (unless the pot is specially designed for self watering).

Luckily, most pots come with holes in the bottom. If you see one you want to buy that doesn't have holes, ask the salesperson if she will drill them for you. Many garden centers offer that service.

7. Plant in the Wrong Amount of Light

Different plants need different amounts of light. A petunia (shown) likes sun, while a dieffenbachia likes shade. But how much sun is enough for sun plants? The rule of thumb is at least four to six hours of direct sun a day. See pages 20 - 21 for more information on light.

Container Gardens are Different From...

Container Gardens are Easier than Landscape Gardens

It is easier for plants to survive in containers than in the ground, which makes container gardening ideal for beginning gardeners. Since decorative container gardens are normally used for one season, you don't have to worry about long term plant success, which is more difficult. And, they are much easier to plant in containers than digging in your yard!

You also don't have to worry about your native soil if you use the great potting mix I recommend on page 8.

Container Gardens are Fast and Instant

For many years, I owned a landscaping business that renovated home landscapes. I was very familiar with huge projects that took many months or years to complete.

I get a tremendous feeling of accomplishment by finishing a container garden so quickly. I photographed this one shortly after planting.

Planting in the Ground

Container Plants need More Water Than Plants in the Ground

Plants need more water in containers because their roots (which store water) can't grow beyond the limits of the pot. However, with the latest automatic watering systems, this chore does not require anywhere near as much time as in years past. See pages 30 - 31 for ideas on easy watering.

Plant Closer Together in Containers

This was hard for me to get used to. After years of landscaping, I was accustomed to spacing plants so they had room to grow. It is imperative that shrubs, trees, and perennials have enough space to grow appropriately, or they won't thrive.

Decorative container gardens are just the opposite; they are designed for seasonal display. The plants need to be planted quite close together in order to provide a finished product quickly. And it works! I was worried that close planting would kill the plants, but they have thrived!

Plants Cannot Live Forever in the Same Pot

In nature, plant roots grow as much as they want. The top of the plant grows proportionally - it gets larger as the roots grow. If the roots reach a barrier - like the edges of a pot - the plant stops growing. Eventually, the roots fill the pot and the plant goes into a decline.

Nurseries start seedlings in tiny pots and move them into larger ones as the plants grow. If you are keeping plants for a long period, you should do the same.

Some plants can stay in the same pot longer than others, including bromeliads, crotons, and succulents (shown, left).

My Plant Trials

Container Plant Trials

When I decided to write books about container gardens, I had already gained extensive container experience from my landscape design and nursery business. But that was in Florida, and I needed to know what people were doing in other areas in order to write a book that was national in scope.

I traveled all over the US and into Canada to begin research on container gardens. It was quite exciting to see the new plants and containers in so many varying areas. It was also quite enlightening to learn how similar container gardens were - even in areas with quite different climates.

After getting home, I decided to test what I had seen, so I would be able to write about the easiest plants and combinations. I planted thousands of plants in hundreds of different containers, so I could learn the best of the best. By doing it myself, I was able to watch each container combination to see exactly how long it lasted as well as what type of maintenance it required to keep it looking its best.

I started observing butterflies when I first started growing flowers. For some reason, I was fascinated with them. They reminded me of flying flowers. For 10 years, I worked on my screen porch that overlooked my gardens (I was living in south Florida and could work on a porch all year). After leaving Florida for Georgia, I would watch butterflies longer than I would write books! I'm really excited about the opportunity to share my knowledge with you.

Above: Three of the many butterfly plants in this garden, left to right: Pink dragonwing begonias, white 'Odorata' begonias, purple New Guinea impatiens.

Right: A glimpse at my trial gardens. These gardens led me to holding the world's record in plant homicide but also taught me about some really easy plants!

Shopping for Plants

Take this book with you when you go to garden centers. When you see a plant on which you need information, check the index to find the appropriate pages.

This book is limited to plants that are great for containers, so don't expect to see shade trees and evergreen shrubs within its pages. Most container plants are annuals and live only one season. Annuals usually have a much higher percentage of color than long-blooming perennials. Since the purpose of container gardens is largely decorative, annuals are usually the best choice.

I also list plants in the last chapter that are commonly available but might not meet your expectations. That information can save you a lot of time, frustration, and money.

Some Plants Might not Meet Your Expections

I purchased these lovely gerber daisies, thinking they would bloom throughout my growing season, or at least six months or so. Not so. They bloomed for a month and never even set another bud. I thought I had done something wrong until I found out that gerber daisies are supposed to only bloom for a month. Had I known that, I would have bought one plant instead of the six I planted in this pot for $7 each!

But the label didn't say how long the plant bloomed, and the garden center lady told me she thought they bloomed for months. She was wrong.

I had the same experience with the kalanchoe (bottom photo). It looked great the day I planted it but only stayed in bloom for about a month.

Many garden center personnel are encyclopedias of plant knowledge. Others are novices in gardening.

The hardest information to find is how long the plant blooms. So, take this book with you. The plant you are looking for may not be here, but chances are it will.

If you see a plant you like that is not in this book, by all means, ask the garden center personnel. Be sure to ask if they have any personal experience with the plant.

Great Plants That are Hit or Miss

One of my favorite container plants is the petunia. I tried eight different varieties of trailing petunias this past season, and they all did beautifully. I've had great luck with some of the Wave petunias from Pan American Seed as well as the Supertunias from Proven Winners (shown left, at one of their growing facilities in Vancouver).

So, why aren't they blue ribbon plants? Many petunias sold today are unnamed. The label just says 'Petunia.' Quite a few of these died on me. I'm afraid if I classify them as the best of the best, you might end up with one of these bad ones and be quite disappointed.

Erratic Performers

Calibrachoa, or million bells, is one of the hottest and prettiest plants in container gardening. However, when they are good, they are very, very good; and when they are bad, they are horrid!

I'm not sure why. Probably, some of the new ones haven't been tried in certain climates and might not like it there. Eventually, they will sort themselves out. For best results, use a tried-and-true brand like Proven Winners. I've had good results with all of their plants. But don't expect even the best calibrachoa to live more than a few months.

Once again, take this book with you to your garden center so you will have a better shot at assessing your risk with certain plants. In many instances, they are so inexpensive that cost is not an issue. However, it is important that both new gardeners and serial plant killers have successful gardening experiences. So, stick with the blue-ribbon plants if you fall into either of those categories.-

Plants Last Longer in Large Containers

Plants in larger containers are easier to care for than those in smaller ones. They live longer because their roots have more room to spread. And they require less water because there is more room for water storage. The mixed flowers (below) have a shorter lifespan and require more frequent waterings than the mixed flowers in the larger container, right.

Below: The plants in these white planters (Michael Carr Designs) lasted much longer - a full six months - than they would have lasted in smaller containers. The lantana attracts the butterflies, while the caladiums and purple Persian shield accent the arrangement. *See pages 120 to 121 for more information.*

Right: Plantings include Mona lavender for the centerpiece surrounded by yellow gaillardia and red petunias. The container is a full 20 inches wide (inside diameter).

Use Centerpieces for Mixed Plantings

Plant the tallest plant in the middle and smaller ones around it. What could be easier! We call the big plant the centerpiece. In this case, the centerpiece is a penta plant, which is a great butterfly magnet. It is surrounded by torenia. I've seen bumblebees disappearing into the center of torenia! They like the pollen that much!

Characteristics of Good Centerpieces

❖ A centerpiece can be any type of plant as long as it remains taller than the surrounding plants for the life of the arrangement.

❖ Choose a plant that is full, or combine several tall, skinny plants together so the centerpiece doesn't look too skinny.

❖ Be sure the centerpiece likes the same growing conditions (light, temperature, water) as the smaller plants that go around it.

Left: Blue salvia makes a great centerpiece because of it's vertical shape. Shrimp plants fill the middle layer and red pentas fill the front edge. These plants are like candy to butterflies!

Understand Light

Different plants need different amounts of light. A petunia likes sun, while a dieffenbachia likes shade. But how much sun is enough for sun plants? The rule of thumb is at least four to six hours of direct sun per day for sun plants. In other words, if your petunia just gets two hours of sun with shade the rest of the day, it will not do well.

If you put a plant that just likes shade in the sun, the leaves and flowers will burn. And, shade is more complicated than sun. It's pretty easy to tell whether your area is in sun; but, shade is trickier. Many plants are quite sensitive to varying degrees of shade - light, medium, and dense. Sit in the same location you are considering for a container and look around.

This colorful combination from Busch Gardens in Tampa thrives in full sun and attracts lots of butterflies. It is planted with yellow California daisy, blue scaevola 'Blue Wonder' and white daisies.

Light Shade

Look up, and you will see about 20-30% leaves and the rest sky. The trees are planted farther apart in light shade than in medium shade. Look down, and notice many types of plants growing. Look around, and see many patches of sky from any direction.

Plants that grow well in light shade also thrive in part-sun, part-shade situations - provided the sun is in the morning hours. If your area gets sun all afternoon, choose plants that tolerate full sun.

Medium Shade

Look up, and you will see medium shade from trees. Look for about 50% or more of sky. Look down, and see ferns or other shade plants growing. Look around, and see more trees but not much open sky on the south or west sides. Sun from the south or west is strong and too much for most medium shade plants.

Fewer plants grow in medium shade than dense shade, but your choices are still wide enough to make a great, colorful container.

Dense Shade

Look up, and you will see the dense shade of very thick trees or the roof of a building. Less than 30% of the sky is visible. Look down and see almost nothing growing, except possibly a few weeds. Look all around, and you will still see very little sky but rather more thickly-leafed trees or buildings.

Many plants thrive in light to medium shade. Dense shade, however, is a difficult situation. Most flowering plants require more light than dense shade provides. Stick to plants you find in the house plant section of your garden center for dense shade situations.

What is Side Planting?

Baskets with Holes in Them!

Side-planted containers have holes in the sides that allow you to plant into the sides as well as the top for an instant look. They are ideal for attracting butterflies because they accomodate a lot of different plants. And remember - butterflies love variety.

They are nothing short of spectacular! Look for hanging baskets, window boxes, living wall planters - plus beautiful baskets supported on column kits, as shown below.

These containers not only look great when planted but also stand the test of time. See Chapter 5 for many examples from my garden that looked great on planting day and lasted a full seven months - with a ten day run of temperatures over 100 degrees!

Side-planted basket on a border column kit.

Side-planted window box. See pages 108 - 109 for more info on this planting.

Side-planted living wall planter

Planting Side-Planted Containers

As Easy as 1-2-3!

Step 1: Add soil up to the first hole. Wet the root balls of the plants, and squeeze them. Slide the root balls through the holes.

Step 2: Plant the centerpiece.

Step 3: Plant the edge plants.

After - Just one week after planting! This basket is planted with dragonwing begonias, coleus, and creeping Jenny. The begonias attract the butterflies.

Planting a Small Container

Step 1

Put some potting mix in the bottom of a pot with holes in it to ensure drainage. Without drainage, most plants die. If the holes are really large, cover with a layer of rock, coffee filter, or plastic screen to keep potting mix from escaping.o see how much potting mix you'll need, hold the largest plant in the center so the top of the mix is about an inch below the top of the new pot. Remove the plant, and adjust the soil to reach that level. Be sure to use top-quality potting mix with a brand name you trust. Do not use garden soil or top soil because these soils are too heavy and can kill the plants.

Step 2

To take the plant out of its pot, hold it upside down, and pull the pot off the root ball. If it resists, squeeze the sides of the pot and try again, or cut the pot off with garden shears.

If the roots are tightly wound in a circle, the plant is root-bound. It will grow better if you separate the roots. Untangle the roots slightly by breaking the tight circle apart. Repeat this action all around the root ball.

Step 3

Place the centerpiece plants in the middle of the container. These three dianthus make a full grouping. They are placed very close together, with root balls touching.

Check the level of the potting mix, and adjust it accordingly. Remember, you want the top of the root balls about an inch below the top of the new pot.

Step 4

Place the edge plants (in this case, coleus and torenia) around the centerpiece. Lean them out slightly, so you won't see soil from the top edge when the pot is done. Add more potting mix under these plants, if necessary, to keep all the root balls even on top.

Be sure to tilt the plants out a little, and keep the tops of their root balls even with the centerpiece. If they are not perfectly filled in, they will grow quickly!

Step 5

Once all the plants are placed, fill in any open spots between the root balls with potting mix. Don't pile the potting mix up around the stems or the plants could die It is all right for the root ball to be planted high, meaning slightly above the potting mix.

Sprinkle the fertilizer I describe on page 46 top of the potting mix. Apply the amount specified on the fertilizer box. If the mix already has fertilizer in it, you can skip the extra fertilizer now if you like. However, I have not found a potting mix with fertilizer that lasts the life of the plants, so I add some of my fertilizer anyway.

Step 6

Move the container to its final resting place before watering because it is lighter without the extra water. Water the container thoroughly and evenly (in a gentle stream with a watering can or hose nozzle) until you see water coming out of the drainage holes. After the pot has drained, add potting mix wherever it has settled. Enjoy! Your butterflies will love the nectar from the purple dianthus and the blue torenia!

Planting a Large Container

Step 1

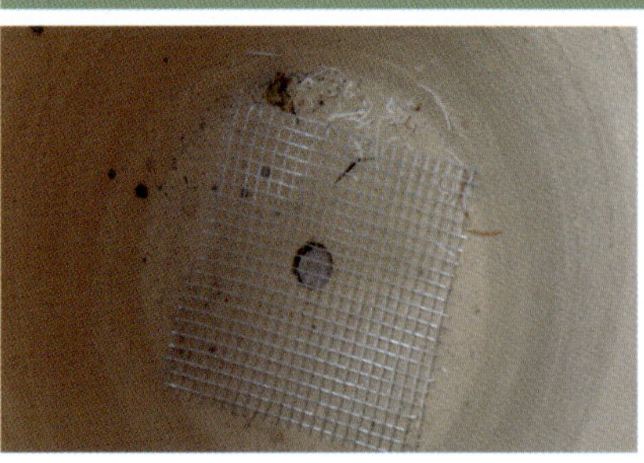

Check to be sure the pot has a drainage hole in the bottom to ensure drainage. Without drainage, most plants die. If the holes are really large, like this one, place some screening in the bottom to keep the gravel (step 2) from escaping through the hole.

It's a good idea to check for holes in the bottom of pots before you buy them. If they are missing, most garden centers will drill them for you before you take them home.

Step 2

Cover the screening with a layer of rock (an inch or two) to keep the potting mix from stopping up the drain hole. Sometimes the hole will clog anyway, so check the pot periodically to see if there is standing water in the top. If so, tilt the pot and have someone stick a screwdriver through the bottom of the drain hole to clear the clog.

Once the rock is in place, cover it with some water-permeable weed cloth or a coffee filter to keep the potting mix from escaping through the drain hole.

Step 3

To see how much potting mix you'll need, hold the plant in the center so the top of the mix is about an inch below the top of the new pot. Remove the plant, and adjust the potting mix to reach that level.

In tall pots like these, I use potting mix throughout the pot if I am planting long-term plants, like the variegated false agaves I'm using here. If I'm planting short-lived plants, like annuals, I fill the bottom half with organic mulch (which is much cheaper than potting mix).

Check the level of the potting mix, and adjust it accordingly. Remember, you want the top of the root balls about an inch below the top of the new pot.

Step 4

Take the plant out of the plastic nursery pot, and loosen the roots if they have grown in a circle. Place the plant on top of the potting mix. Add more potting mix in between the pot and the root ball, along the sides of the pot. Be sure to leave about an inch or so between the top of the potting mix and the rim of the pot to keep the water from overflowing when you apply it. Don't pile the potting mix up around the stems or leaves or the plant could die It is all right for the root ball to be planted high, meaning slightly above the potting mix.

Sprinkle the fertilizer I describe on page 284 on top of the potting mix. Apply the amount specified on the fertilizer box. If the mix already has fertilizer in it, you can skip the extra fertilizer now if you like. However, I have not found a potting mix with fertilizer that lasts the life of the plants, so I add some of my fertilizer anyway.

Step 5

Once all the plants are placed, fill in any open spots between the root balls with potting mix. Don't pile the potting mix up around the stems or the plants could die It is all right for the root ball to be planted high, meaning slightly above the potting mix.

Sprinkle the fertilizer I describe on page 46 top of the potting mix. Apply the amount specified on the fertilizer box. If the mix already has fertilizer in it, you can skip the extra fertilizer now if you like. However, I have not found a potting mix with fertilizer that lasts the life of the plants, so I add some of my fertilizer anyway.

Fertilizer

New Fertilizer is a No Brainer: Just Apply Once

Fertilizer is one of the most important components of blue ribbon plants and easy container gardens. Without fertilizer, the plants will slowly turn yellow and decline.

I have only found one fertilizer that works perfectly every time. And it is forgiving. If you use too much, it doesn't burn the plants. It also is excellent for the environment, winning the Gulf Guardian Award from the EPA Gulf of Mexico Program Partnership.

This fertilizer is slow-release, meaning its little pellets release the nutrients over a period of time. It is a great improvement over the liquids you apply weekly with a hose sprayer! However, there are many slow-release products on the market. I have tested every one I could get my hands on, and none come close to this one. Some either don't last as long or don't have all the nutrients plants need. Others release all their nutrients at once if there is a lot of rain, burning the plants.

This fertilizer lasts nine months in 'average' conditions. If you see the plants yellowing a bit, just add some more. Sprinkle it on top of the potting mix, following the instructions on the label.

Many potting mixes also include fertilizer. I haven't found one yet that lasts long, so I add this one at planting time as well. This fertilizer is available at www.kinsmangarden.com.

Look for These Ingredients on the Label

I have killed many plants with the wrong fertilizer. I have also been through fertilizers that simply didn't make the grade. They included some but not all of the elements a plant needs. Weird, hard-to-diagnose nutritional deficiencies developed that were time consuming, annoying, and definitely not easy.

Plants are like people - they need lots of different nutrients to keep them alive. If you have a vitamin deficiency, you might get quite sick. Same thing for a plant. Learn to read the fertilizer label to make sure it includes *all* the nutrients your plants need. Most fertilizers include nitrogen, phosphorus (phosphate), and potassium (potash). Most, including some of the best-selling brands, don't include the micronutrients that plants need. So look for boron, copper, iron, manganese, and magnesium as well. Do not buy a product that doesn't include these micronutrients, or your plants could suffer later.

All of the containers in this book were fertilized once at planting time with my fertilizer. This container features a jatropha in the center, surrounded by crotons, coleus, and creeping Jenny. Jatropha is a fabulous butterfly magnet.

Watering Basics

General

Watering takes the most time of any container garden chore. Plants in containers need more water than plants in the ground because their root systems are smaller, and the roots are where plants store most of their water. The root system of a plant in the ground is three times the diameter of the plant. Not so for container plants - the roots are only as large as the container.

I was pleasantly surprised by the watering needs of side-planted containers. Prior to using them, I was concerned that the coco fiber liner would not hold water for long. I pictured myself permanently standing next to a container pouring water on it! Luckily, that was not the case. Read these two pages to learn what it took me hundreds of trials to master.

Check out the nozzle on the watering wand shown, left. This nozzle diffuses the water, so you don't blow the little plants right out of the pots. The same effect comes from a nozzle that fits directly on the hose. I like the hose nozzles that have a lot of different settings, so I can use a gentle stream for soaking a container or a strong stream for cleaning a patio.

How to Tell When a Plant Needs Water

Water when you see signs of wilt, or the soil feels dry to the touch. Use your finger to test the soil. Push it into the soil about an inch or so. Low-water plants, like cacti and succulents, need less water and can go longer with dry soil.

Knowing when to water is very important because many container plants die from overwatering. If the plant looks wilted and the soil has been wet for several days, the plant is drowning and will probably die. It has a fungus. You might try a fungicide if the plant is very important to you.

How Much Water to Apply

Water thoroughly with each application. The biggest watering mistake people make is to give the plant just a little bit of water. That is the same as giving a person dying of thirst just a teaspoonful of water! Soak the plant thoroughly until you see a steady stream of water coming out of the bottom of the pot. A slow soaking is better than a fast hit with the hose because it allows the roots time to absorb the water.

Factors That Affect Water Use

- **Sun or shade.** Plants use one-third to one-half as much water in shade than in full sun.
- **Temperature.** Plants use more water when the temperatures are high.
- **Wind.** Plants in windy areas require more water than plants in calm areas.
- **Reflections from walls.** If you have a light-colored wall facing south with no shade, you may have to plant succulents to take the reflected heat if you live in a very hot climate.
- **Soil.** Good-quality potting mix usually includes peat moss, which holds water better than cheaper, sandy soils.
- **Plant type.** Plant species vary in their need for water. Impatiens, for example, need much more water than cactus.
- **Container size.** Large containers with small plants require much less water than small containers filled to the brim with large plants.
- **How long the plant has been in the container.** As plants age in containers, their roots fill the pot, leaving less space for water.

Chapter 2

How to Attract Butterflies

This chapter include lots of tips to entice butterflies to come to your container gardens. To attract butterflies, feed them! To keep them around, feed their young. This chapter shows you how.

<u>It's important to understand when you can expect to see butterflies.</u> On my deck here in north Georgia, I plant my containers in early May. I see lots of pollinators, mainly bumblebees, right away. Shortly after, the skipper butterflies arrive. It's not until mid-July to early August that the big, glamorous swallowtails arrive, plus some smaller beauties like the sulfers and buckeyes. The black and tiger swallowtails come every day once they've found my flowery deck! I've seen them spend up to five hours at a time there, both feeding and resting no more than three feet from my living room windows.

The easiest way to see when butterflies reach your location is to google it.

Opposite and above: Swallowtail butterflies

Blue Ribbon Plants and Combinations

Many Annuals Bloom for the Entire Growing Season

Annuals that bloom for the entire growing season are wonderful for butterflies. I have spent decades watching to see which ones attract the most butterflies. If you want a lot of butterflies, plant many different kinds of flowers because they like variety, just like we do. You wouldn't want to eat the same meal all the time. I call these easiest of these annuals 'Blue Ribbon Plants.'

Characteristics of Blue Ribbon Plants

- ❖ Dependable. Perform the same way every year.
- ❖ Require little to no trimming
- ❖ Adjust to most climates
- ❖ Live a long life - at least the four to six months of your growing season
- ❖ Fare well with little pest susceptibility.
- ❖ Have an established record - it's been around for enough years to fully understand it.
- ❖ Blooms continuously for a minimum of five to six months.

Top 7 Blue-Ribbon Pollinator Annuals (based on observation)

Blue Salvia

Celosia

Lantana

New Guinea impatiens

Pentas

Trailing torenia

Wax begonias

To Feed Your Butterflies

Blue Ribbon Annuals for Butterflies

Angelonia | Begonias, dragon wing | Begonias, wax | California daisy | Celosia

Coleus* | Creeping Jenny* | Crotons* | Dichondra | Gomphrena

Impatiens | Lantana | Melampodium | Pentas | Persian shield*

Salvia, blue | Salvia, red | Scaevola | Shrimp plant | Torenia

* *Used for leaf color only - doesn't attract butterflies. I love a touch of leaf color in many of my container gardens.*

Great Container Perennials and Shrubs...

Annuals Bloom Longer Than Perennials & Shrubs

Both native and exotic annuals bloom much longer than perennials and shrubs. However, the best of the reblooming shrubs now bloom almost as long as annuals.

Look for Shrubs & Perennials with Long Bloom Periods

Many of our favorite shrubs and perennials used to bloom for a very short time, usually a few weeks. But, breeding from hybridizers has produced plants with much longer bloom periods. Many are called 'rebloomers.'

Also, many breeders are producing perennials and shrubs that are much smaller than most. Look for small rebloomers that would fit in a pot. Some great small rebloomers that butterflies love include: Perennial salvias, coneflower, shrub lantana, firebush, and hydrangeas (panicle and lacecap varieties), to name a few.

'Little Quick Fire' Hydrangea is a great choice for butterflies. Stick to panicle and lacecap varieties for lots of butterflies.

Don't Write Off Butterfly Bushes Quite Yet!

The original butterfly bushes were quite invasive, meaning they would reproduce way too much. Since none of us want to ruin our native forests, breeders introduced sterile butterfly bushes, which don't spread. I tried the 'Lo & Behold' series from Proven Winners. It's wonderful, and has the reputation as one of the longest-blooming shrubs you can grow, blooming from mid-summer to frost. Its small size (2' tall by 2' to 3' spread) makes it ideal for containers. Plus, there's a smaller one called 'Lo & Behold 'Pink Micro Chip' that's even smaller. And I don't know of another plant species that attracts more butterflies than butterfly bushes.

Some Great, Long-Blooming Perennials

Agastache 'Blue Fortune'

Look for long-blooming perennials. And always try local natives first, since they are naturally adapted to your area. Here are some suggestions:

Agastache
Astilbe
Coneflower
Coreopsis
Gaillardia
Perennial salvias
Phlox
Shasta daisy
Yarrow

Native is Always Best

Yarrow has a very large native range. It is native to North America, Asia, and Europe.

Native plants occur naturally without human interaction. Or, plants that have existed in a particular area since before 1492 are natives. Native plants naturally support wildlife better than introduced plants.

Always look for native plants first. Check out the website of the Xerces Society. They have a number of valuable resources for native butterfly gardening.

Also, check out the native plant nurseries in your area. the PlantNative website includes a list of native plant nurseries and sources for native plants.

I look forward to a time when natives are much more available in small, 4″ to 6″ pots that are ideal for containers - and priced lower than they are now. I would also love to see more natives available at local and chain-store garden centers. There isn't a native plant nursery within 45 minutes of my house!

To Keep Your Butterflies Around, Feed Their Young.

Butterflies feed on nectar, which comes from most flowers. However, their young larva (look like caterpillars) require different plants - plants where they where they can eat the leaves. So if you want your butterflies to stick around, plant some larval host to feed their young.

While butterflies are not particularly picky about what nectar in the variety of flowers they choose for a drink, young larva will accept only a leaves from very specific plants.

Monarch caterpillar and butterfly on milkweed

Larval Host Plants for 10 Common Butterflies

Black Swallowtail: Parsley, dill, carrot tops, Queen Anne's lace, fennel, turnips

Cloudless Sulphur: Legumes such as cassia and senna plants, partridge pea, alfalfa, clovers

Common Buckeye: Snapdragon, false foxglove, plantains, ruellia and more

Gulf Fritillary: Passionflower

Monarch: Milkweed

Morning Cloak: Deciduous tree leaves like willow, elm, hackberry, aspen, and hawthorne to name a few

Painted Lady: Thistle, mallow, hollyhock, sunflower, aster, red clover, legumes and more

Spicebush Swallowtail: Sweet bay, sassafras, tulip tree, spicebush

Tiger Swallowtail: Leaves of many woody plants, esp. trees & shrubs in the rose, magnolia, and poplar families.

Viceroy: Willow, poplar trees, some fruit trees

***Important Note:** Be sure to know which butterfly species live in your local area before purchasing a larval host plant. If you plant a larval host plant for a butterfly that isn't already in your native area, it won't attract them.

You should also know when to expect the butterflies. The best source of such localized information is Google.

Six Easy Larval Host Plants for Containers

Above, left: Dill foliage. Right, Black swallowtail caterpillar munching on dill.

Above, left: Fennell foliage. Right, Black swallowtail caterpillar munching on fennel.

Above, left: Parsley foliage. Right, Black swallowtail caterpillar munching on parsley.

Monarchs are Endangered, so Please Plant Milkweed.

Asclepias tuberosa
Butterfly weed
Plant profile: Page

Asclepias incarnata
Butterfly weed
Plant Profile: Page

Asclepias curassavica
Butterfly weed
Avoid this one!

❖ Milkweed is the larval host plant of monarch butterflies. There are 30 species of native milkweeds that are host plants for monarchs in the US. They don't have to bloom to feed the caterpillars.

❖ Stick to native varieties like butterfly weed (*Asclepias tuberosa*) shown above left and swamp milkweed (*Asclepias incarnata)* shown above center. I was able to order both varieties from Etsy (online vendor). They are hard to find in garden centers but worth the trouble of online ordering because they both grow really well in containers and attract monarchs like crazy!

❖ Take care with *Asclepias curassavica*, shown upper right. It hosts a parasite that can be debilitating to butterflies and shorten their lifespan. However, entomologists are learning new things about monarchs and milkweed, so check online sources before banishing this one.

❖ All parts of all varieties of milkweed are toxic if eaten or touched. I found this out after 20 years of growing milkweed with no problems whatsoever, so all people are not affected by it. If you are concerned, don't eat it and wear gloves while handling the plant.

Know When Specific Butterflies Frequent Your Area

All species of butterflies won't be hanging around your deck all spring, summer, and fall. Monarchs, for example, migrate across country. They appear at my house in Georgia in the fall. So, I have my milkweed plants fat and happy in anticipation of their arrival. The black swallowtail's first generation of butterflies emerge between late April and early June. The second generation appears in late summer. Eastern tiger swallowtails are present from April though October, July is considered the height of butterfly season, but it varies by location.

Choosing Larval Host Plants

❖ Find out which butterflies frequent your area. Choose the larval host plants for butterflies specific to that location. It's futile to grow a larval host plant for a butterfly that never comes within a thousand miles of your house!

❖ Lots of larval host plants grow quite large, like passionflower vine. I grow it in a container, shown right.

❖ Remember that plants don't grow as large in containers as they grow in the ground. Plus, you can plant large plants in containers - haven't you ever seen trees planted in large pots?

❖ I purchased milkweed plants that grow four to six feet large when planted in the ground. When growing in 12" diameter pots, they only grew about 30" tall.

Have Enough Host Plants to Feed Tons of Caterpillars

When a butterfly lays its eggs on a larval host plant, LOTS of caterpillars appear once the eggs hatch. And these caterpillars devour larval host plants. Once, they ate all of a milkweed plant the day the eggs hatched. I was terrified of running out of food for the babies, so I drove to two garden centers and bought lots of milkweed plants. Now, I use these guidelines:

❖ Plant at least three milkweed plants. All three can be the same variety. This summer, I have four planters filled with three different varieties of milkweed. I know I can attract monarchs with only one variety, but I wanted to try the other two to see how they would do. My milkweed plants are fat and happy by the time the monarchs arrive at my Georgia location - in September. Remember that milkweed plants don't need to bloom to feed monarch caterpillars since they just eat the leaves.

❖ One passionflower vine has always been enough for my caterpillars. Plant it only if you live in an area where gulf frittillary and/or zebra longwings live.

❖ One pipevine is also enough . Plant only if you live in an area with pipevine swallowtails.

❖ Plant one parsley and one fennel if you live in an area with black swallowtails. If you run out, it's easy enough to stop by the grocery store to get more.

I am planting these larval host plants for butterflies that frequent my location. Be sure to choose the larval host plants that attract butterflies found in your area.

Larval Host Plants

Buying Tips

I have had great luck attracting butterflies by planting larval host plants. This year, I decided to plant several milkweed varieties, as well as passionflower and dutchman's pipe. I only found one variety of milkweed at local garden centers. None of the other plants were available locally.

I found all of the plants on Etsy, a website. I dealt directly with their growers, and they were great! I'm sure there are many other websites that sell larval host plants.

Plant Larval Host Plants Alone

I plant larval host plants alone, one variety per pot. Since the plants will get devoured if the butterflies lay their eggs on them, you don't want them in a mixed arrangement. One devoured plant will ruin the beautiful effect of the healthy, blooming plants. Plus, caterpillars literally cover the larval host plant when the eggs hatch. Understand that larval host plants don't have to bloom to feed the caterpillars.

Three varieties of milkweed planted on my deck.

Left: Passionflower vine; Right: Pipevine

Entice Butterflies With Bright-Colored Flowers

Butterflies are attracted to red, yellow, orange, pink, and purple flowers. I decided to use these bright colors in a side-planted window box. Here's the result. It includes red, orange, and yellow celosia, teamed with hot pink pentas; yellow, red and purple calibrachoa and purple heliotrope. 24" side-planted window box from kinsmangarden.com.

Even a simple planting, like this Lechuza planter featuring blue salvia, yellow marigolds, and red begonias, will please your butterflies.

More Butterfly Basics

Attracting Hummingbirds

Hummingbirds prefer tubular-shaped flowers because they fit their beak. However, I notice them drinking from most of the flowers in my container gardens. Butterflies prefer a flower with a broad surface. They can land on it to feed. I notice butterflies most on my penta and lantana plants but they drink from the rest of them as well. Attract both with a garden filled with different flower shapes and colors.

Avoid Pesticides

This should be obvious! Pesticides kill bugs, and butterflies are bugs. I will sometimes very carefully use a fungicide on plants that need it. So far, my pollinators keep thriving around that plant, however, I am incredibly careful. Spray early in the morning when the wind is minimal.

Butterflies Like Variety

Would you like to eat the same food all the time? Of course not, and neither do the butterflies. Plant as many different flowering plants as your space allows.

Butterflies Require Sunlight

Butterflies are cold-blooded and need sunlight to warm the muscles they need to fly. So set your butterfly containers in a spot with as much sunlight as possible.

Give Your Butterflies a Drink

Butterflies need water, just like humans. I simply put a saucer of water on my deck railing, with just a little water in it. You can also create a 'puddling' area. Check out 'puddling' online.

Dealing with Bees & Wasps

Bees like a lot of the same flowers as butterflies. They both prefer flat, open blooms with big petals. Watch them and notice how they balance on a flower while they are drinking. Luckily, bees and butterflies share food without conflict. I have read that bees prefer white, yellow, and blue blooms, but I see them feasting on bright red and pink blooms as well. Some people, (0.4 percent of the population, I have heard) who are allergic to bee stings and should be concerned when they see any kind of bee.

Wasps - particularly yellow jackets - are fairly aggressive. They frequent my garden, but I've never been stung by one in the garden area. However, I am cautious. Here are some tips to keep from getting stung:

❖ Don't take drinks into the garden. I drank a beer on my deck. When I washed out the glass, I found a dead yellow jacket in the bottom of it. Luckily, I didn't swallow it. If you swallow a bee or wasp, call 911 immediately.

❖ Don't wear shirts with large, floppy sleeves when watering. A bee could get confused and fly up your sleeve.

❖ Look for wasp nests, particularly on the underside of decks. However, don't kill any wasp that shows up in your garden! They are pollinators, too! I have never been stung by a wasp in my butterfly gardens, and I see them all the time. Somehow, they seem to understand that I am an essential cog in their machine because I keep all their flowers alive. However, take care of nests. I have been stung multiple times in natural areas from stepping on yellow jacket nests. So, I have a pest control company come over each summer to look for nests within my garden area. So far, they haven't found any.

❖ Wear shoes when outside, for obvious reasons.

❖ Plant flowers that don't attract bees. According to Paul Thomas with the University of Georgia, these include cultivars of dianthus, geraniums, chrysanthemums, some zinnias and many roses. This is almost impossible for me because I want as many flower species as I can find in my butterfly garden!

❖ I have a lot of yellow jackets, other wasps, and bumblebees in my butterfly gardens. I feel a great affection for bumblebees - we get along famously. I'm a little careful around wasps, but so far, so good!.

Chapter 3

Butterfly Plants in Traditional Pots

I call all planters that aren't side-planted 'traditional pots.'

Materials for traditional pots include clay, glazed pottery, plastic, and many synthetics. The variety is endless! Be sure to shop at lots of great garden centers, as well as online suppliers, before choosing your pots.

The larger the pot, the longer the plants live. You will see that fact demonstrated over and over in this chapter. And the difference is dramatic. A plant placed in a small pot might last a month or two. Plant it in a larger planter and it could last six months.

I, along with my assistants, planted all of these and carefully monitored them for their entire lifespan. That way, I could report the results to you.

Left: Swallowtail feasting on scaevola 'Blue Wonder'

Above, left: Tiger swallowtail feasting on pentas
Avove, center: Swallowtail and lantana
Above, right: Swallowtail and zinnias

Combine Food with Flowers

I love tucking in some edibles with the flowers in container gardens, and the butterflies don't mind at all! This mixed flower arrangement would have lasted longer in a larger pot, but the plants thrived for three months in this small bowl. And the butterflies loved the scaevola.

Black-eyed Susan
1 plant from a 4" pot
Plant Profile: Page 155

Tiny Chili Peppers
1 plant from a 4" pot

Scaevola 'Blue Wonder'
2 plants from 4" pots
Plant Profile: Page 165

Creeping Jenny
2 plants from 4" pots
Plant Profile: Page 157

Cultural Information

Light: Full sun

Season: These plants thrive in high heat and will take temperatures from 65 to 90 degrees.

Lifespan: This combination lasted 10 weeks. The plants would have lived longer in a larger container.

Care: Fertilize on planting day with a slow-release mix described on pages 28 - 29. Repeat if the leaves look yellowish or washed-out, although the fertilizer should last from 6 - 9 months.

Water: Water thoroughly if the plants show signs of wilt, or the soil feels dry when you push your fingertip into the potting mix. I watered this one every day in midsummer (after it was about a month old) and every other day in cooler weather. See pages 30 - 31 to learn about watering shortcuts.

Trouble Shooting: No problems at all

Planting Plan: Plant the black-eyed Susan along the back of the bowl. Plant the pepper in the center. Surround with the scaevola and creeping Jenny. Be sure to plant in good-quality potting mix, not garden soil, top soil, or potting soil, which can kill your plants.

Container: Bright blue bowl, 14" across

Beautiful, Pastel Flower Bowl

This combination was planted with large plants shortly before this photo was taken. The butterflies loved it. However, the plants were so large compared with the size of the pot that the arrangement only lasted about six weeks. But the low cost, coupled with the ease of planting made it well worth the time and money. Use larger pots for longer-lasting arrangements.

White Snapdragons
3 plants from 4" pots
Plant Profile: Page 165

Pink Petunias
3 plants from a 4" pots
Plant Profile: Page 163

White Verbena
2 plants from a 4" pots
Plant Profile: Page 166

Blue Violas
3 plants from a 4" pots
Plant Profile: Page 165

Cultural Information

Light: Light shade to full sun

Season: These plants thrive in temperatures ranging from 45 to 85 degrees.

Lifespan: 6 weeks. These plants last longer in larger containers.

Care: Fertilize on planting day with a slow-release mix described on pages 28 - 29. Repeat if the leaves look yellowish or washed-out, although the fertilizer should last from 6 - 9 months.

Water: Water thoroughly if the plants show signs of wilt, or the soil feels dry when you push your fingertip into the potting mix. I watered this one every day in midsummer (after it was about a month old) and every other day in cooler weather. See pages 30 - 31 to learn about watering shortcuts.

Trouble Shooting: No problems at all

Planting Plan: Easy. Simply plant the snapdragons in the middle, and surround them with the smaller plants, alternated.

Caution: The snapdragons all stop blooming at the same time while new buds are forming. The flowers re-appear in about a month later. This factor causes them to miss a ribbon.

Container: 20" x 8" bowl

Butterflies Love Bright-Colored Flowers

Like all annual plantings in small containers, this arrangement didn't last too long, only eight weeks. However, the flowers proved to be butterfly magnets. They feasted mainly on the purple lantana and the snapdragons. Even though the snapdragons go in and out of bloom, the butterflies were fine with feasting on the rest of the flowers.

Snapdragons
2 plants from 6" pots
Plant Profile: Page 165

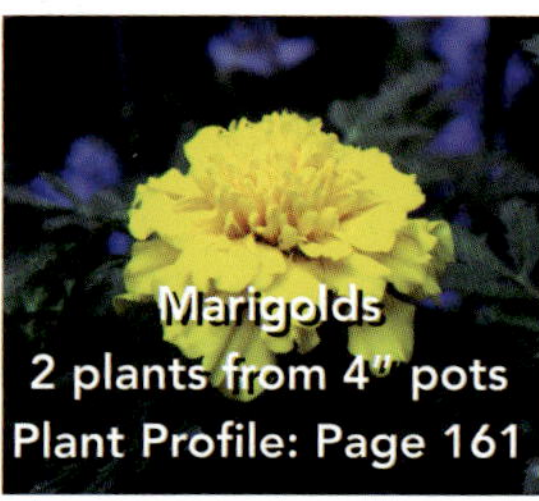

Marigolds
2 plants from 4" pots
Plant Profile: Page 161

Violas
2 plants from 4" pots
Plant Profile: Page 165

Lantana
2 plants from 4" pots
Plant Profile: Page 161

Cultural Information

Light: Light shade to full sun

Season: These plants thrive when temperatures are over 45 and under 85 degrees.

Lifespan: These plants lived for about 3 months.

Care: Fertilize on planting day with a slow-release mix described on pages 28 - 29. Repeat if the leaves look yellowish or washed-out, although the fertilizer should last from 6 - 9 months.

Water: Water thoroughly if the plants show signs of wilt, or the soil feels dry when you push your fingertip into the potting mix. I watered this one every day in midsummer (after it was about a month old) and every other day in cooler weather. See pages 30 - 31 to learn about watering shortcuts.

Trouble Shooting: The marigolds and snapdragons bloom more if old flowers are removed.

Planting Plan: Simply plant the snapdragons in the middle and surround them with the other plants.

Container: 15″ white bowl

1ST Simple Planting

This planting earns a blue ribbon (defined on pages 34 - 35) because all the plants are easy to grow and never go out of bloom. This bowl is deeper than the bowls seen on the previous six pages. This extra depth provided enough extra soil to keep the plants thriving for a full 10 weeks. It would have lived for five to six months in larger containers. All three plants attract butterflies.

Shrimp Plant
2 plants from 6" pots
Plant Profile: Page 165

Pentas
4 plants from 4" pots
Plant Profile: Page 163

Torenia
2 plants from 4" pots
Plant Profile: Page 166

Cultural Information

Light: Light shade to full sun

Season: These plants thrive in high heat and will take temperatures down to 32 degrees.

Lifespan: Ten weeks in this container. These plants would thrive for 5 - 6 months in a larger container.

Care: Fertilize on planting day with the slow-release mix described on pages 28 - 29. Repeat if the leaves look yellowish or washed-out, although the fertilizer should last from 6 - 9 months.

Water: Water thoroughly if the plants show signs of wilt, or the soil feels dry when you push your fingertip into the potting mix. I watered this one every day in midsummer (after it was about a month old) and every other day in cooler weather. See pages 30 - 31 to learn about watering shortcuts.

Trouble Shooting: No problems at all

Planting Plan: Easy. Simply plant the shrimp plants along the back of the container, the pentas in the middle, and the torenia along the front edge.

Container: Blue bowl, 16" wide by 7" high

Great Colors for Butterflies

When shopping for bright-colored flowers, I was lucky enough to find all these plants at the same garden center. The coneflower is a perennial that I'll plant in my garden in the fall. I planted these in mid-July, in a year of record-breaking heat, and they did well with temperatures in the 87 - 90 degree range.

Angelonia
4 plants from 6" pots
Plant Profile: Page 154

Coneflower
4 plants from 6" pots
Plant Profile: Page 156

Celosia
4 plants from a 4" pot
Plant Profile: Page 156

Lilac Vinca
3 plants from 4" pot
Plant Profile: Page 165

Pink Vinca
3 plants from 4" pots
Plant Profile: Page 165

Cultural Information

Light: Light shade to full sun

Season: These plants thrive in high heat and will take temperatures down to 40 degrees.

Lifespan: In this bowl (16"w x 6" h), this plant mix lasts about 2 months. In a larger planter, they would last the entire growing season.

Care: Fertilize on planting day with a slow-release mix described on pages 28 - 29. Repeat if the leaves look yellowish or washed-out, although the fertilizer should last from 6 - 9 months.

Water: Water thoroughly if the plants show signs of wilt, or the soil feels dry when you push your fingertip into the potting mix. I watered this one every day in midsummer (after it was about a month old) and every other day in cooler weather. See pages 30 - 31 to learn about watering shortcuts.

Trouble Shooting: No problems at all

Planting Plan: Plant the angelonia along the back edge, and the celosia in the center front. Add the coneflowers and tuck the vincas around the edge of the bowl. Be sure to plant in good-quality potting mix, not garden soil, top soil, or potting soil, which can kill your plants.

Container: Navy blue bowl, 16" wide x 6" high

Color Impact from Only Two Flowers

What a great idea for cobalt blue pots! This simple arrangement of red double impatiens surrounded by yellow calibrachoa (or million bells) is all this pot needs to become a striking combination. Although the double impatiens are fabulous container plants, the calibrachoa is an erratic performer, so the arrangement didn't rate a ribbon. Some calibrachoa varieties I tried did quite well, while others only lasted a month or two.

If you find a good calibrachoa cultivar, this arrangement is very easy to care for. The impatiens filled in quickly, but the calibrachoa were planted small and took a few months to trail over the edge of the pot.

Red Double Impatiens
3 plants from gallon pots
Plant Profile: Page 160

Yellow Calibrachoa
8 plants from 4" pots
Plant Profile: Page 155

Cultural Information

Light: Light shade is ideal for most areas. Takes full sun in cool, short, frost-free days, like the winter in south Florida or the summers in Maine.

Season: Plant when temperatures vary between 40 and 90 degrees. The calibrachoa do not do well in higher heat.

Lifespan: About 4 months in this container if the calibrachoa is a dependable cultivar.

Care: Fertilize on planting day with the slow-release mix I describe on page 8. Repeat if the leaves look yellowish or washed out.

Both flowers drop a lot. The impatiens are particularly hard to remove from pavement.

Water: Water thoroughly when plants show signs of wilt, or the the soil feels dry when you push your fingertip into the potting mix. I watered this one every three days in spring and every day in the heat of summer. Impatiens require quite a bit of water. See pages 30 - 31 to learn about watering shortcuts.

Troubleshooting: These flowers drop a lot, which require a lot of clean-up if you use them on pavement.

Planting Plan: Easy. Plant the impatiens in the middle and surround them with calibrachoa. Be sure to plant in good-quality potting mix, not garden soil, top soil, or potting soil, which can kill your plants. Other important planting tips are shown on pages 24 - 27.

Container: I bought this pot from a roadside vendor.

Traditional Flowers

While both of these plants attract butterflies, the pentas are one of the pollinator superstars. They attract more butterflies than almost any other flower I plant. They bloom from spring to fall in all but the coldest areas. Both plants look better and produce more flowers when deadheaded (trimming off the dead flowers). And they are great choices for areas that are really hot. Plus, the plumbago lives as a shrub in zones 9 through 11. The combination misses a blue ribbon because the plumbago takes breaks from blooming.

Pink Pentas
3 plants from 4" pots
Plant Profile: Page 163

Plumbago
1 plant from a 10" pot
Plant Profile: Page 164

Cultural Information

Light: Light shade to full sun

Season: Grow when the temperatures range from 75 to over 100 degrees. Although the plumbago lives in temperatures that are much lower, it doesn't bloom unless it is quite warm.

Lifespan: About 4 months in this container. These plants would live longer in a larger container.

Care: Fertilize on planting day with the slow-release mix I describe on page 8. Repeat every six to nine months or if the leaves look yellowish or washed-out. The pentas bloom more if the old blooms are removed.

Water: Water thoroughly if the plants show signs of wilt, or the soil feels dry when you push your fingertip into the potting mix. I watered this one every day in midsummer (after it was about a month old) and every other day in cooler weather. See pages 30 - 31 to learn about watering shortcuts.

Trouble Shooting: No problems at all

Planting Plan: Easy. Plant the plumbago in the center, along the back edge of the pot. Fill in the front with the pentas. Be sure to plant in good quality potting mix, not garden soil, top soil, or potting soil, which can kill your plants.

Container: Global Pottery's *Fleur De Lis* in French Yellow (16"H x 13"W). Shop for it at www.globalpottery.com.

1ST Pastels in a Coordinated Pot

Three of my favorite plants - shrimp plant, dragon wing begonia, and torenia - coordinate well with this attractive container. And butterflies love all three. However, the short life of the torenia (three months), coupled with the small size of the container, limit the lifespan of this arrangement to only two to three months.

They offer some advantages, however - adapting to a wide range of temperatures and blooming through the hottest summers or coolest springs. But, be sure to protect them from freezes.

Cultural Information

Light: Light shade is ideal. Takes full sun in cooler temperatures.

Season: This plant combination is tolerant of a wide range of temperatures, from mid-40's to the low-100's, which means spring until fall in most areas.

Lifespan: Only 2 to 3 months in this small (10" wide) container. The shrimp plant and begonia will last at least six months in a larger container.

Care: Fertilize on planting day with the slow-release mix I describe on 28 - 29. Repeat if the leaves look yellowish or washed out. No trimming is necessary, but the shrimp plant blooms more if the dead flowers are removed.

Water: Water thoroughly when the plants show signs of wilt or the soil feels dry when you push your fingertip into the potting mix (see pages 30 - 31). I watered this one every day in midsummer and every other day in cooler weather. This plant mix would require less water if planted in a larger container.

Troubleshooting: No problems. This is a wonderful, trouble-free arrangement.

Planting Plan: Plant the shrimp plant in the middle with the torenia on either side. The dragon wing begonia rests in the center, along the front edge of the pot. Be sure to plant in good-quality potting mix, not garden soil, top soil, or potting soil, which can kill the plants.

The arrangement was planted for immediate fullness by dipping the root balls in water to reduce their size.

Container: Global Pottery's *Square Planter* from "The Country Home Collection" (10"H x 10"W) from www.globalpottery.com.

Note about Torenia: Upright torenia lasts about three months. Trailing torenia lasts for up to one year.

Dragon Wing Begonia
2 plants from 4" pots
Plant Profile: Page 154

Shrimp Plant
1 plant from a 10" pot
Plant Profile: Page 165

Blue Upright Torenia
2 plants from 4" pots
Plant Profile: Page 166

Variety is the Spice of Life for Butterflies

This plant grouping features five plants that attract butterflies. I chose these plants not only because I want the butterflies to enjoy it, but also because I wanted to try limiting the colors to different shades of pink, purple, and silver. The cleome only lived for about a month or two, but its pretty blooms are worth the trouble. The rest of the plants last about two to three months.

Cleome
1 plant from a 6" pot
Plant Profile: Page 156

Pink Petunias
5 plants from 6" pots
Plant Profile: Page 163

Salvia coccinea 'Brenthurst'
1plant from a 6" pot

Mona Lavender
1 plant from a 6" pot
Plant Profile: Page 162

Helichrysum 'Icicles'
4 plants from 4" pots
Plant Profile: Page 160

Purple Calibrachoa
2 plants from 6" pots
Plant Profile: Page 155

Cultural Information

Light: Light shade to full sun

Season: Temperatures between 40 and 85 degrees

Lifespan: Other than the cleome, which lasted about a month, the other plants lasted 2 - 3 months.

Care: Fertilize on planting day with a slow-release mix described on pages 28 - 29. Repeat if the leaves look yellowish or washed-out, although the fertilizer should last from 6 - 9 months.

Water: Water thoroughly if the plants show signs of wilt, or the soil feels dry when you push your fingertip into the potting mix. I watered this one every day in midsummer (after it was about a month old) and every other day in cooler weather. See pages 30 - 31 to learn about watering shortcuts.

Trouble Shooting: No problems at all

Planting Plan: Start with the largest pot. Plant the cleome along the back edge. Alternate the petunias and calibrochoa along the edge. For the middle pot, plant the Mona lavender in the middle. Alternate the 'Icicles' and petunias along the edge. For the small pot, plant the salvia along the back and the 'Icicles' in front. Surround the 'Icicles' with petunias. Be sure to plant in good-quality potting mix, not garden soil, top soil, or potting soil, which can kill your plants.

Container: International Pottery Allliance 'Senzhen Planter' in sesame green. 12", 15", and 19" wide.

Neon Colors Attract Butterflies

These gorgeous, large, shiny red planters are from the Michael Carr garden covered in chapter 5. Persian shield and shrimp plants form the centerpieces. Yellow lantana, purple heliotrope, and creeping Jenny are planted below. Both the pentas and the lantana are butterfly magnets. All the plants are blue-ribbon plants except the heliotrope, which blooms sporadically. The blue ribbon plants lasted the entire season.

Persian Shield
3 plants from 4″ pots
Plant Profile: Page 163

Shrimp Plant
2 plants from 4″ pots
Plant Profile: Page 165

Red Pentas
3 plants from 4″ pots
Plant Profile: Page 163

Yellow Lantana
6 plants from 4″ pots
Plant Profile: Page 161

Heliotrope
6 plants from 4″ pots
Plant Profile: Page 160

Cultural Information

Light: Light shade to full sun

Season: These plants thrive in high heat and will take temperatures down to 40 degrees.

Lifespan: 5 - 6 months.

Care: Fertilize on planting day with a slow-release mix described on pages 28 - 29. Repeat if the leaves look yellowish or washed-out, although the fertilizer should last from 6 - 9 months.

Water: Water thoroughly if the plants show signs of wilt, or the soil feels dry when you push your fingertip into the potting mix. I watered this one every day in midsummer (after it was about a month old) and every other day in cooler weather. See pages 30 - 31 to learn about watering shortcuts.

Trouble Shooting: No problems at all

Planting Plan: Plant the larger plants (shrimp plants and Persian shield) along the back of the planters, tucking the smaller plants along the front edge.

Container: Michael Carr Pottery

Bright Pots Combined with Bright Flowers

These large, bright pots are planted on top of 'Surdiva Sky Blue' scaevola (planted in the ground), another hit with the butterflies. Once again, I love planting in large pots because the roots of the plants have room to grow. This space allows the plants to live much longer than in smaller planters. Check out the rest of this garden in Chapter 5.

Ruellia 'Purple Showers'
2 plants from 6" pots
Plant Profile: Page 164

Shrimp Plant
4 plants from 6" pots
Plant Profile: Page 165

Purple Pentas
6 plants from 4" pots
Plant Profile: Page 163

Coleus
6 plants from 4" pots
Plant Profile: Page 156

Cultural Information

Light: Light shade to full sun

Season: These plants thrive in high heat and will take temperatures down to 40 degrees.

Lifespan: 5 months

Care: Fertilize on planting day with a slow-release mix described on pages 28 - 29. Repeat if the leaves look yellowish or washed-out, although the fertilizer should last from 6 - 9 months.

Water: Water thoroughly if the plants show signs of wilt, or the soil feels dry when you push your fingertip into the potting mix. I watered this one every day in midsummer (after it was about a month old) and every other day in cooler weather. See pages 30 - 31 to learn about watering shortcuts.

Trouble Shooting: No problems at all

Planting Plan: Plant the larger plants along the back edge. Tuck the smaller ones along the front edge.

Container: Michael Carr Pottery

Comment: I'm not crazy about Ruellia 'Purple Showers' in containers because it doesn't bloom continuously and grows tall and lanky.

Plants Last Longer in Larger Pots

Like the red planters on the previous four pages, these gorgeous pots came from Michael Carr Pottery (see Chapter 5 for more details). The plants loved the large size of the pots and they lasted the full growing season. The butterflies loved the flowers! Notice the unique canna lily with flowers of different colors. Canna lilies are the host plant for brown skipper butterflies.

Celosia 'Intenz Lipstick'
4 plants from 4" pots
Plant Profile: Page 156

Coleus
4 plants from 4" pots
Plant Profile: Page 156

Canna 'Cleopatra'
1 plant from a 10" pot
Plant Profile: Page 155

Cultural Information

Light: Light shade to full sun

Season: These plants thrive in high heat and will take temperatures down to 32 degrees.

Lifespan: This planting lasted 5 months.

Care: Fertilize on planting day with a slow-release mix described on pages 28 - 29. Repeat if the leaves look yellowish or washed-out, although the fertilizer should last from 6 - 9 months.

Water: Water thoroughly if the plants show signs of wilt, or the soil feels dry when you push your fingertip into the potting mix. I watered this one every day in midsummer (after it was about a month old) and every other day in cooler weather. See pages 30 - 31 to learn about watering shortcuts.

Trouble Shooting: No problems at all

Planting Plan: Plant the canna lilies along the back of the planter, tucking in the coleus in front. One celosia plant is planted in each of the small planters. Be sure to plant in good-quality potting mix, not garden soil, top soil, or potting soil, which can kill your plants.

Container: Michael Carr Pottery

Chapter 4

Butterflies Love Side-Planted Containers!

Side-planted containers fit four times as many plants (per square foot) as traditional planters. So, if you have a small deck or patio, you can attract more butterflies with these floriferous planters! See pages 78-79 for more information.

Side-planted containers are planted both on the top and in the side. This side planting allows for much fuller baskets than traditional baskets and also accommodates a lot more plants. The baskets are supported by chains or posts. Side-planted window boxes and living walls are also available.

Side-planted baskets are my favorite planter for butterflies because they hold so many plants. While a traditional, 16" planter holds about 6 plants, a 16" side-planted basket holds about 25! And, amazingly enough, the plants in the basket will live for an entire growing season. I've never figured out exactly why, but my theory is the holes on the sides allow more oxygen to the roots of the plants, which causes them to last longer.

Opposite: A Morning Cloak butterfly on coneflowers

Above, right: Buckeye butterfly on marigolds

Above, left: Painted Lady butterfly on coneflower

Planting the Basket: It's Easy!

Empty basket: The holes in the sides of the baskets allow mature plants to be pushed through the sides for an instant look. This is a 16-inch, basic basket on a decorative patio stand.

Step 1: Add about two inches of potting mix. Wet the root balls of the plants, and squeeze them. Slide the root balls though the holes.

Step 3: Add potting mix as needed and plant the centerpiece and along the back edge of the basket.

Step 4: Tuck another row of annuals along the front and side edges. Add soil as needed and fertilize.

See a planting video on youtube.com/Pamelacrawford-landscape-videos. Look for 'How to Plant a Spectacular Basket.'

Displaying: Hang from a Chain...

1. Either hang from a chain or mount on a basket or border column kit, shown on next two pages.

Displaying: Mount on a Border Column Kit...

Or Place on A Basket Column Kit

These baskets can be displayed on border columns, which go into the ground (opposite page), or basket columns, that go into pots (this page). Both supports feature a disc that is attached to the top of the columns to support the basket.

The border columns are either 4" x 4" square wooden posts or 2" round metal posts. The 4" x 4" posts come in 4 heights: - 30", 36", 42", and 48". The metal posts are 36" high with 12" extensions.

The basket column kits come with a 36" metal post and a 12" extension. All are available from kinsmangarden.com.

See an instructional video on youtube.com/@Pamelacrawford-landscape/videos. Look for 'How to Install Supports for Container Gardens.'

Side-Planted Window Boxes

The planters on this deck were planted with edibles and flowers. The window boxes (this page and opposite) were brimming with gomphrena, begonias, lantana, and melampodium. Tomatoes were planted in the top. Sweet basil and melampodium fill the blue column.

Side-Planted Containers Fit More Plants And...

This Basket Accomodates Four Times as Many Plants as a Traditional Planter, Attracting Many More Butterflies.

I have a small deck and I expect a lot from it. The living area of my house overlooks it, so I see my deck garden all day long. And I want lots of butterflies, which means I need lots of plants. Side-planted containers are ideal for that because they accommodate more plants than traditional planters.

Look at the large, green pot on this page. It takes up about four square feet and accommodates approximately nine plants. The 16" double, side-planted basket (above it) fits about 25 plants, or 4 times as many plants! More flowering plants attract more butterflies!

The basket is mounted on a basket column kit for large pots (all side-planted products are available at kinsmangarden.com.)

Right: Basket mounted on column kit and planted with a California daisy, begonias, melampodium, creeping Jenny, and gomphrena.

Pots from Pacific Home & Garden

Attract More Butterflies Than Traditional Planters

My Favorite Planting Ever!

This arrangement features more different plants than I usually use and the butterflies loved it. I frequently watched multiple butterflies drinking from these flowers at the same time. Remember that butterflies like a variety of flowers, and this combo filled the bill. The pot is huge, a full 28" across, which added to its impact. It missed a blue ribbon because of the underperforming heliotrope.

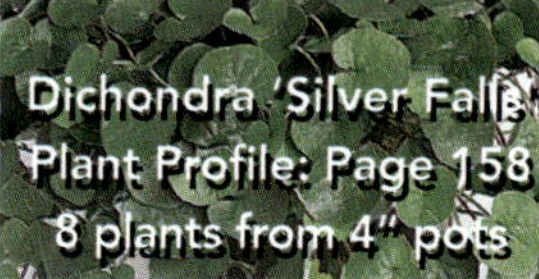

Cultural Information

Light: Light shade to full sun

Season: These plants thrive in the hot Georgia summer from May to October. They take temperatures down to 32 degrees.

Lifespan: 5 - 6 months

Care: Fertilize on planting day with a slow-release mix described on pages 28 - 29. Repeat if the leaves look yellowish or washed-out, although the fertilizer should last from 6 - 9 months.

Water: Water thoroughly if the plants show signs of wilt, or the soil feels dry when you push your fingertip into the potting mix. I watered this one every day in midsummer (after it was about a month old) and every other day in cooler weather. See pages 30 - 31 to learn about watering shortcuts.

Trouble Shooting: No problems at all

Planting Plan: The dramatic pink dracaena forms the centerpiece the side plants - lantana, torenia, scaevola, and dichondra 'Silver Falls' are alternated in the side holes and along the top edge.

Container: The spectacular, turquoise pot is from Michael Carr Designs. It measures a full, 28" across. The basket is a 16" double side-planted basket, #ZCK16 from kinsmangarden.com. The pole is a basket column kit for large pots, #ZPSBK. Purchase from kinsmangarden.com.

Planting: See a planting video on youtube.com/@Pamelacrawford-landscape/videos. Look for 'How to Plant a Spectacular Basket.'

Colors Your Butterflies will Love!

These planters are part of a garden I called my 'Crayon Box Garden.' I mixed all different pot colors along a railing. The colors of the flowers follow suit with the bright-colored theme. And yes, the butterflies loved it! The red verbena went in and out of bloom. The rest of the flowers bloomed continuously all summer long. The only thing I would change is to use a larger centerpiece in the basket. This planting merits a blue ribbon (defined on pages 34 to 35) because it lasted a full six months with very little care.

Celosia, Mixed Colors
Plant Profile: Page 156
11 plants from 4" pots

Blue Salvia
Plant Profile: Page 164
6 plants from 4" pots

Red Verbena
Plant Profile: Page 166
6 plants from 4" pots

Yellow Lantana
Plant Profile: Page 161
6 plants from 4" pots

Trailing Angelonia
Plant Profile: Page 154
9 plants from 4" pots

Cultural Information

Light: Light shade to full sun

Season: These plants thrive in high heat and will take temperatures down to 40 degrees.

Lifespan: Plants lasted about 4 - 6 months.

Care: Fertilize on planting day with a slow-release mix described on page 28 - 29. Repeat if the leaves look yellowish or washed-out, although the fertilizer should last from 6 - 9 months.

Water: Water thoroughly if the plants show signs of wilt, or the soil feels dry when you push your fingertip into the potting mix. I watered this one every day in midsummer (after it was about a month old) and every other day in cooler weather. See pages 30 - 31 to learn about watering shortcuts.

Trouble Shooting: No problems at all. However, I would have preferred that the verbena bloomed more.

Planting Plan: Assemble the basket column kit for large pots before planting. Then, sit the 16" double basket on a table. Add a little potting mix. Dip the root balls of the side plants (angelonia, small marigolds, and verbena) in water and squeeze them tightly. Slip the root balls through the side holes. Add a bit more soil and plant the large marigolds and angelonia in the center. Surround by more of the verbena, small marigolds, and angelonia.

Container: Pacific Home & Garden

Planting: See a planting video on youtube.com/@Pamelacrawford-landscape/videos. Look for 'How to Plant a Spectacular Basket.'

Captivating Color

I used a basket column kit for large pots in the largest pot. I experimented with planting the purple angelonia behind large, yellow marigolds, hoping the angelonia would grow taller than the marigolds. It worked! The butterflies loved the combination of bright colors and nectar-filled flowers. Plus, I was surprised at how much the bumblebees liked the wax begonias.

4 Purple Angelonia
Plant Profile: Page 154
9 plants from 4″ pots

8 Marigolds
Plant Profile: Page 161
6 plants from 4″ pots

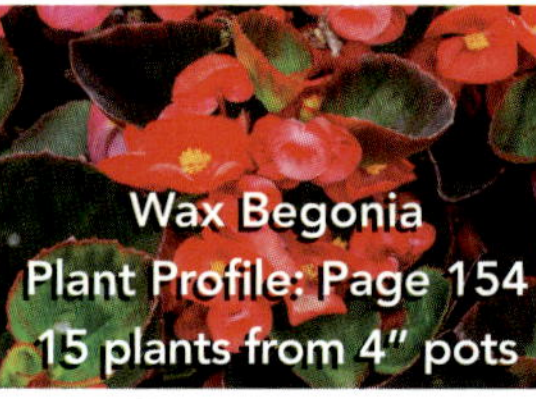
Wax Begonia
Plant Profile: Page 154
15 plants from 4″ pots

Creeping Jenny
Plant Profile: Page 157
4 plants from 4″ pots

Celosia, Mixed Colors
Plant Profile: Page 123
11 plants from 4″ pots

Cultural Information

Light: Light shade to full sun

Season: Anytime temperatures are between 45 degrees and the low 90's.

Lifespan: The marigolds and celosia only lived about three months. The other plants will live six months in containers this size.

Care: Fertilize on planting day with the slow-release mix I describe on pages 28 - 29. Repeat if the leaves look yellowish or washed-out. Trim the dead flowers off the marigolds, and keep the creeping Jenny in the top basket from growing into the blue container.

Water: Water when the plants show signs of wilt or the soil feels dry when you push your fingertip up to your second knuckle into the potting mix. I watered this one every day in midsummer (after it was about a month old) and every other day in cooler weather.

Troubleshooting: No problems

Planting Plan: Assemble the basket column kit for large pots before planting. Sit the basket on a table. Plant the marigolds in the center and the angelonia along the back edge. Alternate the smaller marigolds with the creeping Jenny and the red begonias along the top edge. Plant the celosia in the smaller pots.

Container: The basket is a 16″ single side-planted basket, #ZCK16 from kinsmangarden.com. The pole is a basket column kit for large pots, #ZPSBK. Purchase from kinsmangarden.com.

Planting: See a planting video on youtube.com/@Pamelacrawford-landscape/videos. Look for 'How to Plant a Spectacular Basket.'

Bright Colors in Light Shade

The location of this blue ribbon arrangement (defined on pages 34 - 35) only gets about 3 hours of full sun per day. The rest of the day, it's in light shade. I didn't know if that was enough light for most of these plants and was pleasantly surprised at the wonderful outcome. The orange lantana was the only plant that didn't bloom much in this low light. And the butterflies loved this basket, particularly the pentas.

Red Pentas
Plant Profile: Page 163
1 plant from an 8" pot

Coleus
Plant Profile: Page 156
6 plants from 4" pots

Blue Trailing Torenia
Plant Profile: Page 166
5 plants from 4" pots

Orange Lantana
Plant Profile: Page 161
5 plants from 4" pots

Blue Scaevola
Plant Profile: Page 165
5 plants from 4" pots

Melampodium
Plant Profile: Page 162
5 plants from 4" pots

Cultural Information

Light: Light shade to full sun. Blooms most in full sun.

Season: These plants thrive in high heat and will take temperatures down to 40 degrees.

Lifespan: All these plants are blue-ribbon plants and live about 6 months if planted in May.

Care: Fertilize on planting day with a slow-release mix described on pages 28 - 29. Repeat if the leaves look yellowish or washed-out, although the fertilizer should last from 6 - 9 months.

Water: Water thoroughly if the plants show signs of wilt, or the soil feels dry when you push your fingertip into the potting mix. I watered this one every day in midsummer (after it was about a month old) and every other day in cooler weather.

Planting Plan: Assemble the basket column kit for large pots before planting. Sit the basket on a table, and add a little potting mix. Dip the root balls of the side plants (impatiens, begonias, scaevola, and torenia) in water, and squeeze them tightly. Slip the root balls through the side holes. Add a bit more soil. Plant the large marigolds and angelonia in the center. Surround by more of the verbena, small marigolds and angelonia.

Container: 16" single side-planted basket (ZGVS16) on a basket column kit for large pots (ZPSKB) from kinsmangarden.com.

Planting: See a planting video on youtube.com/@Pamelacrawford-landscape/videos. Look for 'How to Plant a Spectacular Basket.'

My 2nd Favorite Planting Ever!!!!!

I really shopped for the brightest-colored flowers I could find for this basket. I wanted to see how far I could push it with lots of neon-colored varieties. I loved it, and so did the butterflies! Between the butterflies, hummingbirds and bees, there was always some action on this beautiful, blue ribbon combination (defined on pages 34 - 35). The hummingbird came daily and spent a lot of time drinking from these flowers.

'Intenz Classic' Celosia
Plant Profile: Page 156
1 plant from a 8" pot

'Catalina Gilded Grape' Torenia
Plant Profile: Page 166
6 plants from 4" pots

'Compact Tropical Rose' Sunpatiens
Plant Profile: Page 160
6 plants from 4" pots

Surdiva 'Blue Violet' Scaevola
Plant Profile: Page 165
6 plants from 4" pots

Red Wax Begonia
Plant Profile: Page 154
6 plants from 4" pots

Cultural Information

Light: Light shade to full sun

Season: These plants are adaptable to temperatures from 40 degrees to the mid-'s.

Lifespan: 4 - 6 months

Care: Fertilize on planting day with a slow-release mix described on page 28 - 29. Repeat if the leaves look yellowish or washed-out, although the fertilizer should last from 6 - 9 months.

Water: Water thoroughly if the plants show signs of wilt, or the soil feels dry when you push your fingertip into the potting mix. I watered this one every day in midsummer (after it was about a month old) and every other day in cooler weather. See pages 30 - 31 to learn about watering shortcuts.

Trouble Shooting: No problems at all

Planting Plan: Assemble the basket column kit for large pots before planting. Sit the basket on a table and add a little potting mix. Dip the root balls of the side plants (impatiens, begonias, scaevola, and torenia) in water. Squeeze them tightly. Slip the root balls through the side holes. Add a bit more soil and plant the large celosia in the center of the top. Surround it with the smaller plants.

Container: 16" single side-planted basket (ZGVS16) on a basket column kit for large pots (ZPSKB) from kinsmangarden.com.

Planting: See a planting video on youtube.com/@Pamelacrawford-landscape/videos. Look for 'How to Plant a Spectacular Basket.'

Five Different Butterfly Plants

This arrangement is a great choice for flower lovers. And, it attracts lots of butterflies and bumblebees. The plant choice would have been simplified had I used just one color of torenia, but I had some left over from another basket, so I used two colors instead. The only early fatality was the zinnia centerpiece, which died from a fungus. I replaced it with a tall grass.

Zinnia
Plant Profile: Page 166
1 plant from a 1-gal. pot

Dark Purple Torenia
Plant Profile: Page 166
6 plants from 4" pots

Melampodium
Plant Profile: Page 162
11 plants from 4" pots

Dark Red Torenia
Plant Profile: Page 166
6 plants from 4" pots

Wax Begonia
Plant Profile: Page 154
11 plants from 4" pots

Cultural Information

Light: Full sun to light shade. Since many wax begonias are grown for shade, be sure to choose those that fit your light situation.

Season: Spring through fall for most areas. This plant mix takes temperatures from about 38 degrees to the low 90's in full sun. In light shade, it withstands higher temperatures into the high 90's.

Lifespan: 4 - 5 months in this container

Care: Fertilize on planting day with a slow-release mix. Repeat if the leaves start looking yellowish or washed-out. Remove the dead flowers from the zinnias if you feel energetic!

Water: Water when the plants show signs of wilt or the soil feels dry when you push your fingertip up to your second knuckle into the potting mix. I watered this one every day in mid-summer (after it was about a month old) and every other day in cooler weather.

Planting Plan: Alternate the melampodium, torenia, begonia, and melampodium in the side holes. Add soil. Plant the zinnia in the center. Tuck in the same 4" plants along the top edge.

Container & Support: The basket is a 16" double, side-planted basket, #ZCK16 from kinsmangarden.com. The pole is a basket column kit for large pots, #ZPSBK. Purchase from kinsmangarden.com

Planting & Supporting: See a planting video on youtube.com/@Pamela-crawford-landscape/videos. Look for 'How to Plant a Spectacular Basket.' Learn how to install the post at the same Youtube address. Look for 'How to Install Supports for Container Gardens.'

Cheerful Look for Butterflies

1ST

This is one of my favorite designs because it looks so happy! The combination of pink, yellow, and light blue is a sure-fire winner of a blue ribbon (defined on pages 34 - 35). The textural differences between the flower shapes adds to the interest. In addition, this is a easy combination to grow. The petunias bloomed for about three months. The rest of the plants bloomed for a full, seven-month period!

California Daisy
Plant Profile: Page 155
3 plants from 6" pots

Petunia
Plant Profile: Page 163
10 plants from 4" pots

Lantana
Plant Profile: Page 161
10 plants from 4" pots

Blue Scaevola
Plant Profile: Page 165
10 plants from 4" pots

Cultural Information

Light: Light shade to full sun

Season: These plants thrive in high heat and will take temperatures down to 40 degrees.

Lifespan: The petunias lasted about 3 months. The other plants lasted about 7 months.

Care: Fertilize on planting day with a slow-release mix described on pages 28 - 29. Repeat if the leaves look yellowish or washed-out, although the fertilizer should last from 6 - 9 months.

Water: Water thoroughly if the plants show signs of wilt, or the soil feels dry when you push your fingertip into the potting mix. I watered this one every day in mid-summer (after it was about a month old) and every other day in cooler weather. See pages 30 - 31 to learn about watering shortcuts.

Trouble Shooting: No problems at all

Planting Plan: Alternate the petunias, lantana, and scaevola in the side holes. Add soil and plant the daisy in the top, centered. Tuck another layer of the petunias, lantana, and scaevola along the top edge.

Container and Support: 16" double side-planted basket (ZGVD16) mounted on a ZGBC40 border column kit from kinsmangarden.com.

Planting & Supporting: See a planting video on youtube.com/@Pamela-crawford-landscape/videos. Look for 'How to Plant a Spectacular Basket.' Learn how to install the post at the same Youtube address. Look for 'How to Install Supports for Container Gardens.'

Tomatoes & Flowers

I planted a tomato in the top of this basket and alternated colorful flowers around it. The tomatoes tasted great, but the plant died in about 10 weeks. The rest of the blue-ribbon plants took over the space once occupied by the tomato and lived all season long, for a total of 6 months! And the butterflies loved the bright colors.

Tomato
1 plant from a 4" pot

Lantana
Plant Profile: Page 161
10 plants from 4" pots

Blue Scaevola
Plant Profile: Page 165
10 plants from 4" pots

Dragonwing Begonia
Plant Profile: Page 154
10 plants from 4" pots

Cultural Information

Light: Light shade to full sun

Season: These plants thrive in high heat and will take temperatures down to 32 degrees.

Lifespan: This tomato lasted about 2 - 3 months. I cut them off at the soil line when they were done, and the other plants over nicely. They lasted about 4 - 5 months.

Care: Fertilize on planting day with a slow-release mix described on pages 28 - 29. Repeat if the leaves look yellowish or washed-out, although the fertilizer should last from 6 - 9 months.

Water: Water thoroughly if the plants show signs of wilt, or the soil feels dry when you push your fingertip into the potting mix. I watered this one every day in midsummer (after it was about a month old) and every other day in cooler weather. See pages 30 - 31 to learn about watering shortcuts.

Planting Plan: Easy. Simply plant the tomatoes, peppers, and basil in the center of the pot, along the back edge. Be sure to plant in good-quality potting mix, not garden soil, top soil, or potting soil, which can kill your plants.

Container and Support: 16" double side-planted basket (ZGVD16) mounted on a ZGBC40 border column kit from kinsmangarden.com.

Planting & Supporting: See a planting video on youtube.com/@Pamelacrawford-landscape/videos. Look for 'How to Plant a Spectacular Basket.' Learn how to install the post at the same Youtube address. Look for 'How to Install Supports for Container Gardens.'

One of My Easiest

1ST

This beautiful basket was one of the easiest to maintain in my trials, easily winning a blue ribbon (defined on pages 34 - 35). Although impatiens require more water than most other plants, we kept the basket under oak trees. Since plants require much less water in shade, we only watered it every day in the hottest part of the Georgia summer. Butterflies will venture into light shade if they are tempted from a nearby, sunny area.

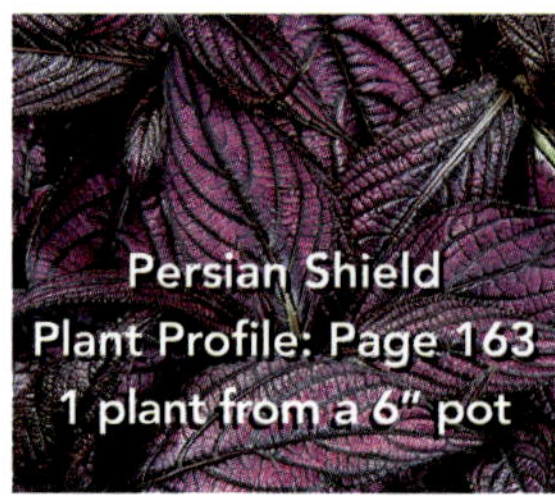

Persian Shield
Plant Profile: Page 163
1 plant from a 6" pot

Wax Begonia
Plant Profile: Page 154
12 plants from 4" pots

Red Impatiens
Plant Profile: Page 160
6 plants from 4" pots

Purple Impatiens
Plant Profile: Page 160
6 plants from 4" pots

Cultural Information

Light: Medium shade to full sun in cooler weather. Impatiens take sun in hot weather but don't like it. They also will drive you crazy with water needs in too much sun and heat. Most take sun until the temperatures hit the low 90's. If it's hotter than that, or summer days are quite long where you live, keep them in the shade.

Season: Spring through fall in most areas

Lifespan: 3 - 5 months in this container but lives longer in cooler weather, although it lasted four months for me in a hot Georgia summer!

Care: Fertilize on planting day with a slow-release mix described on page 28 - 29. Repeat if the leaves look yellowish or washed-out, although the fertilizer should last from 6 - 9 months.

Water: Water thoroughly if the plants show signs of wilt, or the soil feels dry when you push your fingertip into the potting mix. I watered this one every day in midsummer (after it was about a month old) and every other day in cooler weather.

Planting Plan: Alternate the two colors of impatiens in the side holes. Add soil and plant the Persian shield in the center. Tuck the white begonias along the top edge.

Container: 16" single side-planted basket (ZGVS16) mounted on a ZGBC36 border column kit from kinsmangarden.com.

Planting & Supporting: See a planting video on youtube.com/@Pamela-crawford-landscape/videos. Look for 'How to Plant a Spectacular Basket.' Learn how to install the post at the same Youtube address. Look for 'How to Install Supports for Container Gardens.'

Pastels

All of the flowers in this arrangement provide nectar for butterflies. And the arrangement is a feast for human eyes as well. The tiny alyssum flowers show up really well with the neighboring impatiens. The spikey salvia flowers also contrast well with the pink, round flowers of the salvia. Pink, pale blue and white is a can't-fail color scheme.

Geranium
Plant Profile: Page 159
2 plants from 6" pots

Blue Salvia
Plant Profile: Page 164
2 plants from 6" pots

Alyssum
Plant Profile: Page 154
12 plants from 4" pots

Pink Impatiens
Plant Profile: Page 160
9 plants from 4" pots

White Impatiens
Plant Profile: Page 160
9 plants from 4" pots

Cultural Information

Light: Light shade to full sun. However, if your summer is cool, and your days long, keep it in light shade because the impatiens will do better.

Season: These plants do well in temperatures ranging from 35 - 85 degrees.

Lifespan: 4 - 5 months in this container provided the temperatures range from 35 - 85 degrees.

Care: Fertilize on planting day with a slow-release mix described on page 28 - 29. Repeat if the leaves look yellowish or washed-out, although the fertilizer should last from 6 - 9 months.

Water: Water when the plants show signs of wilt or the soil feels dry when you push your fingertip up to your second knuckle into the potting mix. I watered this one every three days because the weather was cool (this one was planted in south Florida in winter) and the basket was in light shade.

Trouble Shooting: No problems at all. This was a wonderful, trouble-free basket.

Planting Plan: Alternate the two colors of impatiens in the side holes. Add potting mix and plant the geraniums and salvia. Tuck the alyssum along the top edge.

Container: #ZGIPS16 single imperial planter from kinsmangarden.com.

Planting & Supporting: See a planting video on youtube.com/@Pamelacrawford-landscape/videos. Look for 'How to Plant a Spectacular Basket.'

Neon Color Lights Up this Window Box

This is one of my favorite all-time window box plantings. And the butterflies loved it. However, I was quite disappointed at it's short, three-month lifespan. It's decline started when the temperatures reached 95 degrees, so I shouldn't complain! Plus, calibrachoa never lasts too long for me. The arrangement was so pretty that I didn't whine too much about the short lifespan.

Geranium
Plant Profile: Page 159
2 plants from 6" pots

Calibrachoa
Plant Profile: Page 155
6 plants from 4" pots

Purple Petunias
Plant Profile: Page 163
6 plants from 4" pots

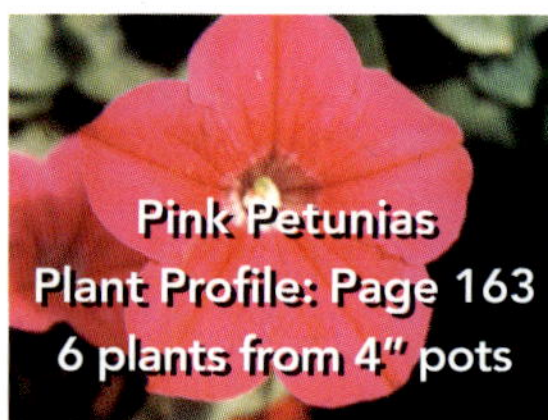

Pink Petunias
Plant Profile: Page 163
6 plants from 4" pots

Cultural Information

Light: Light shade to full sun

Season: These plants do best in temperatures from 40 - 85 degrees.

Lifespan: Three months. Calibrachoa is a relatively short-lived annual. Petunias vary a lot in performance. Buy both plants from brands you trust.

Care: Fertilize on planting day with a slow-release mix described on pages 28 - 29. Repeat if the leaves look yellowish or washed-out, although the fertilizer should last from 6 - 9 months.

Water: Water thoroughly if the plants show signs of wilt, or the soil feels dry when you push your fingertip into the potting mix. I watered this one every day in midsummer (after it was about a month old) and every other day in cooler weather. See pages 30 - 31 to learn about watering shortcuts.

Trouble Shooting: No problems at all

Planting Plan: Alternate the petunias in the side holes. Add potting mix and plant the geraniums along the back edge. Fill in along the top edge with the calibrachoa and a few petunias.

Container: ZWBS24 side-planted window box from kinsmangarden.com.

Hanging & Planting: See 'How to Hang Window Boxes and Wall Pots' on youtube.com/@Pamelacrawford-landscapes/videos. Also, see a side-planting video on youtube.com/@Pamelacrawford-landscape/videos. Look for 'How to Plant a Spectacular Basket.' The planting method is the same for window boxes and round baskets.

Pastel Flowers

This planting really worked well. The cleomes in the center went out of bloom a few times. However, the rest of the plants are blue ribbon plants and bloomed constantly for six months! Butterflies and other pollinators visited these flowers regularly. Remember to stick to blue ribbon plants (page 39) if you want long lasting, easy container gardens.

Pink Wax Begonia
Plant Profile: Page 154
6 plants from 4" pots

'Serena' Angelonia
Plant Profile: Page 154
4 plants from 4" pots

Cleome
Plant Profile: Page 156
3 plants from 1-gal. pots

Scaevola
Plant Profile: Page 165
6 plants from 4" pots

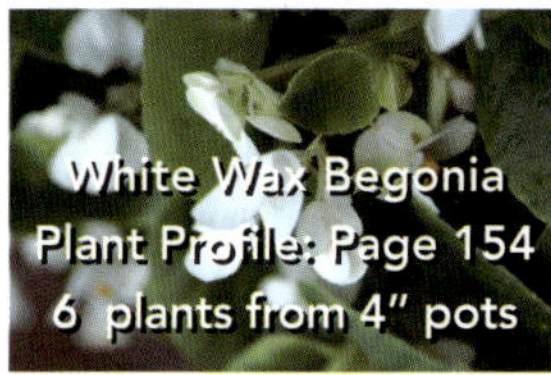
White Wax Begonia
Plant Profile: Page 154
6 plants from 4" pots

Cultural Information

Light: Full sun to light shade

Season: Plant when the temperatures range from 45 degrees to the low 100's. This arrangement tolerates both extremes well.

Lifespan: 5 - 6 months in this large, 36" window box

Care: Fertilize on planting day with the slow-release mix I describe on page 8. Repeat if the leaves look yellowish or washed-out. Trim the scaevola if it gets too long.

Water: Water thoroughly when plants show signs of wilt, or the soil feels dry when you push your fingertip into the potting mix (see pages 30 - 31). Water every three days in spring and every day in the heat of summer.

Troubleshooting: No problems. This was a wonderful, trouble-free arrangement.

Planting Plan: This arrangement was planted with large plants (sizes shown in the photos, left), so it would be full on planting day.

Container: Kinsman's #CLZW36 window box (36"L x 9"W x 9"D). Buy from kinsmangarden.com.

Hanging & Planting: See 'How to Hang Window Boxes and Wall Pots' on youtube.com/@Pamelacrawford-landscapes/videos. Also, see a side-planting video on youtube.com/@Pamelacrawford-landscape/videos. Look for 'How to Plant a Spectacular Basket.' The planting method is the same for window boxes and round baskets.

Fennel, a Host Plant, & Flowers

Fennel is a host plant for the Eastern Black Swallowtail butterfly. Combining it with butterfly nectar flowers is a great way to attract them. From a design standpoint, fennel gives just the right touch with its fine, delicate texture to contrast with the larger leaves of the flowering plants. If the caterpillars eat all the fennel, there are enough other plants to keep the arrangement full.

Fennel
Plant Profile: Page 159
3 plants from 6" pot

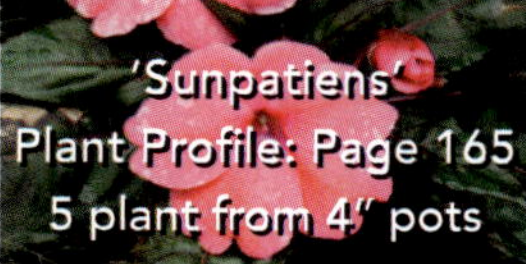

Cultural Information

Light: Light shade to full sun

Season: Spring through fall for most warmer areas. This plant grouping takes temperatures from about 70 degrees to the low 90's.

Lifespan: In this container, 5 - 6 months

Care: Fertilize on planting day with the slow-release mix described on page 28 - 29. Repeat if the leaves look yellowish or washed-out, although the fertilizer should last from 6 - 9 months.

Water: Water thoroughly if the plants show signs of wilt, or the soil feels dry when you push your fingertip into the potting mix. I watered this one every day in midsummer (after it was about a month old) and every other day in cooler weather. See pages 30 - 31 to learn more about watering.

Troubleshooting: No problems at all

Planting Plan: Alternate the lantana, petunias, impatiens, and fennel in the side holes of this side-planted window box. Plant the California daisies in the center of the top, along the back. Plant the blue salvia and cleome on either side of it. Tuck in more of the plants planted in the side holes along the front edge. See the planting instructions for side-planted containers on page 72 to learn the technique.

Container: 36" side-planted window box from www.kinsmangarden.com.

Hanging & Planting: See 'How to Hang Window Boxes and Wall Pots' on youtube.com/@Pamelacrawford-landscapes/videos. Also, see a side-planting video on youtube.com/@Pamelacrawford-landscape/videos. Look for 'How to Plant a Spectacular Basket.' The planting method is the same for window boxes and round baskets.

Blue-Ribbon the Second Time Around

I am always intoxicated by calibrachoa in the garden centers in spring. I planted this window box in early May with lots of calibrachoa (see photo on page 44). As usual, they went into a decline in June. I pulled them out and replaced them with all blue-ribbon plants. After spending the time and money on planting a window box, it's really nice to have it last all season long!

Blue salvia
Plant Profile: Page 164
2 plants from 6" pots

Lantana 'Little Lucky' Orange'
Plant Profile: Page 161
4 plants from 4" pots

Dragonwing Begonias
Plant Profile: Page 154
4 plants from 4" pots

'Catalina Gilded Grape' Torenia
Plant Profile: Page 166
4 plants from 4" pots

'Surdiva Blue Violet' Scaevola
Plant Profile: Page 165
4 plants from 4" pots

Cultural Information

Light: Light shade to full sun

Season: These plants thrive in high heat and will take temperatures down to 40 degrees.

Lifespan: 4 - 6 months

Care: Fertilize on planting day with a slow-release mix described on pages 28 - 29. Repeat if the leaves look yellowish or washed-out, although the fertilizer should last from 6 - 9 months.

Water: Water thoroughly if the plants show signs of wilt, or the soil feels dry when you push your fingertip into the potting mix. I watered this one every day in midsummer (after it was about a month old) and every other day in cooler weather. See pages 30 - 31 to learn about watering shortcuts.

Trouble Shooting: No problems at all

Planting Plan: Easy. Alternate the side and edge plants in the side holes. Add potting mix. Plant the salvia on top, towards the back of the planter. Tuck in another row of plants, alternated, along the top edge. Be sure to plant in good-quality potting mix, not garden soil, top soil, or potting soil, which can kill your plants.

Container: ZWBS24 - 24" window box from kinsmangarden.com.

Hanging & Planting: See 'How to Hang Window Boxes and Wall Pots' on youtube.com/@Pamelacrawford-landscapes/videos. Also, see a side-planting video on youtube.com/@Pamelacrawford-landscape/videos. Look for 'How to Plant a Spectacular Basket.' The planting method is the same for window boxes and round baskets.

1ST Bright-Colored Window Box

The plantings in this window box were a joy to grow because they looked great and attracted a lot of butterflies with very little care. All four of the flowering plants are candy for butterflies. I added the coleus to enhance the overall look, even though it didn't attract butterflies. The pentas attracted the most, although they fed from all the flowers. This arrangement easily wins a blue-ribbon, defined on pages 34 - 35.

Purple Angelonia
Plant Profile: Page 154
2 plants from 4" pots

Coneflower
Plant Profile: Page 156
1 plant from a 6" pot

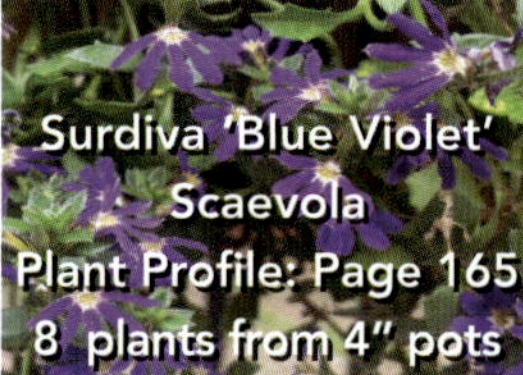

Surdiva 'Blue Violet' Scaevola
Plant Profile: Page 165
8 plants from 4" pots

Colorblaze 'El Brighton' Coleus
Plant Profile: Page 156
8 plants from 4" pots

'Sunstar' Red Pentas
Plant Profile: Page 163
8 plants from 4" pots

Cultural Information

Light: Light shade to full sun

Season: These plants thrive in high heat and will take temperatures down to 32 degrees.

Lifespan: 5 to 6 months. The coneflower will not bloom the entire time..

Care: Fertilize on planting day with a slow-release mix described on page 28 - 29. Repeat if the leaves look yellowish or washed-out, although the fertilizer should last from 6 - 9 months.

Water: Water thoroughly if the plants show signs of wilt, or the soil feels dry when you push your fingertip into the potting mix. I watered this one every day in midsummer (after it was about a month old) and every other day in cooler weather. See pages 30 - 31 to learn about watering shortcuts.

Trouble Shooting: No problems at all

Planting Plan: Alternate the scaevola and coleus in the side holes in the top. Plant the angelonia and coneflower along the back edge. Surround it with the coleus, scaevola, and pentas.

Container: ZWBS24 - 24" window box from kinsmangarden.com.

Hanging & Planting: See 'How to Hang Window Boxes and Wall Pots' on youtube.com/@Pamelacrawford-landscapes/videos. Also, see a side-planting video on youtube.com/@Pamelacrawford-landscape/videos. Look for 'How to Plant a Spectacular Basket.' The planting method is the same for window boxes and round baskets.

Chapter 5

Michael Carr's Butterfly Garden

I frequently work with GardenSmart TV, a PBS show, on either landscape makeover or container gardening shows.

The Michael Carr gardens are the subject of four shows on GardenSmart TV, which broadcasts on PBS. I designed the garden which included over 50 fabulous containers.

The homeowner, Michael Carr, designs pottery for Michael Carr Pottery. The purposes of the garden are to showcase his fabulous pottery, attract butterflies, and provide a beautiful garden spot in his yard.

This garden is host to more pollinators than any other residential garden I have ever seen (except my own)! Although not every single plant attracts butterflies, so many of them do that the garden is loaded with pollinators!

My thanks to Michael, as well as the GardenSmart staff: Jim McCutcheon, Executive Producer, Eric Johnson, Host, and Dettrick Little, Videographer.

Also, thanks goes to Delilah Onofrey of Suntory Flowers; Corrina Murray of Southern Living Plants and Plant Development Services; Christa Steenwyk of Proven Winners Perennials and Walter's Gardens; Natalie Carmolli of Proven Winners Shrubs and Spring Meadow Nursery; and Ball Seed Company. All of these people and their companies provided the plants I requested to make this garden a reality.

All the butterflies on these two pagess are monarchs.

Garden Design & Plant Shopping

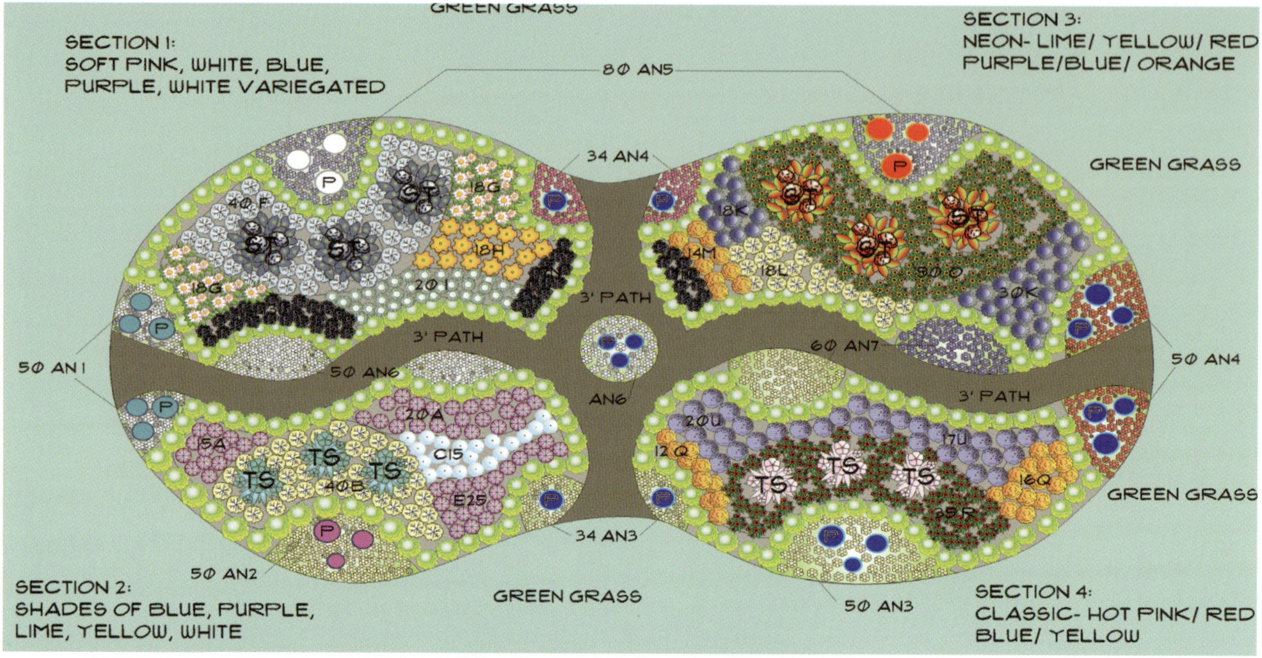
GREEN GRASS
SECTION 1:
SOFT PINK, WHITE, BLUE,
PURPLE, WHITE VARIEGATED
80 AN5
SECTION 3:
NEON- LIME/ YELLOW/ RED
PURPLE/BLUE/ ORANGE
34 AN4
GREEN GRASS
18G
40 F
18H
20 I
18K
14M
18L
30 O
30K
3' PATH
3' PATH
50 AN1
50 AN6
60 AN7
50 AN4
AN6
20A
15A
C15
40B
E25
20U
17U
12 Q
16Q
3' PATH
35 R
GREEN GRASS
34 AN3
50 AN2
SECTION 2:
SHADES OF BLUE, PURPLE,
LIME, YELLOW, WHITE
GREEN GRASS
50 AN3
SECTION 4:
CLASSIC- HOT PINK/ RED
BLUE/ YELLOW

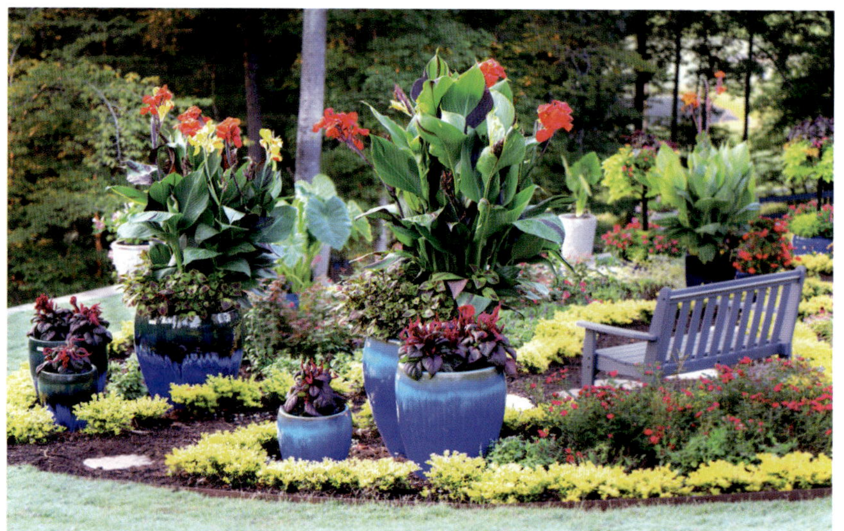

Above: Plan for the garden showing four different sections for four different color schemes.

Left: One of the entries to the garden. *See pages 72 - 73 for more information about the plantings in these containers.*

4 Sections, 4 Color Schemes

Design Features Four Different Sections

Butterflies and bees like a variety of plants. Would you like the same dinner every night? Neither do they, so I decided to use as many different butterfly plants as possible.

Butterflies are also attracted to a lot of diverse colors. So I designed four distinct sections with different color schemes to provide structure for a lot of different butterfly plants.

Section 1. Pastels - pink, white, blue, lavender

Section 2. Dark and light - dark colors contrasted with lime and white

Section 3. Brights - red, yellow, orange, purple

Section 4. Blue, purple and red

Each section is bordered by lime green, which is the go-with-everything garden color. We chose Ilex 'Touch of Gold,' which is the most important plant in the whole garden (from a design standpoint) because it unifies the diverse colors and textures. The bright, lime green color also lights up the garden.

The entry to each section is marked by a pair of planters. Planters also accent the outer edge of the garden, as well as the path.

Good News: Shopping for Plants is a Whole, New Ball Game

Years ago, the biggest challenge of putting together a garden like this was finding the plants. It was completely hit or miss, and you had to drive from garden center to garden center to find what you wanted. It would have taken you the rest of your life to locate these varieties using that method.

Now, you can shop online, which completely opens up your garden choices. I recommend shopping very early in the season, like January. Gardening is growing in popularity, and growers can run out if you wait much past January. The online nurseries I buy from will delay shipment of your plants until it's close to planting time.

However, don't forget your local garden centers. They work hard to have fabulous selections, and you can see the plants before you buy them.

Section 1: Pastel Shrubs & PerennialsPlanted in the Ground

Perennials and Shrubs

Remember your grandmothers hydrangeas that bloomed for a few weeks - if you were lucky? The new, reblooming shrubs and perennials bloom for months on end. I chose long-blooming, pastel-colored flowering shrubs and perennials for planting in the ground in section 1. Annuals were planted in the pots.

Three Color Layers

Tallest layer: Proven Winner's hydrangea, 'Little Quick Fire,' is one the of longest-blooming shrubs I've encountered, blooming non-stop from early until late summer.

Middle layers: Proven Winner's Echinacea 'Price is White' blooms from June to late summer. And the Proven Winners Buddleia 'LO & BEHOLD' series blooms from midsummer until the first frost - plus, unlike many other Buddleias, they are not invasive.

Border: 'Touch of Gold' Holly from Southern Living Plants

Buddleia LO & BEHOLD 'Blue Chip' (Proven Winners)

Buddleia LO & BEHOLD 'Pink Micro Chip' ' (Proven Winners)

Echinacea 'Price is White' (Proven Winners)

Hydrangea 'Little Quick Fire' (Proven Winners)

'Touch of Gold' Holly (Southern Living Plants)

Annuals Planted in the Pots

Top basket: ZGBD16 - 16″ double side-planted basket from kinsmangarden.com.

Basket support: ZBSBK Basket column kit for large pots from kinsmangarden.com.

Centerpiece: Dracaena marginata 'Tricolor'

Basket side and edge plants: Dichondra 'Silver Falls,' Heliotrope 'Marine', Surdiva 'Sky Blue' scaevola (Suntory), lantana 'Little Lucky Hot Pink', Torenia 'Summer Wave Bouquet Gold (Suntory)'

Bottom pot: Angelonia 'Serenita Pink'

Planted in the pots: Persian shield, 'Florida Fancy' caladium, and 'Little Lucky Hot Pink' lantana.

Planted in the ground: Buddleia Lo & Behold 'Blue Chip,' Buddleia Lo & Behold 'Pink Micro Chip,' Echinacea 'Price is White' and Hydrangea 'Little Quick Fire.'

'Touch of Gold' Holly forms the border.

Section 2: Light & Dark Shrubs Planted in the Ground

This section is a study in contrast. I used dark-colored shrubs with very light-colored shrubs. The lime 'Touch of Gold' holly provides a beautiful border.

Three Color Layers:

Tallest: Proven Winner's Viburnum 'Steady Eddy' forms the centerpiece. It features a long bloom period in spring and again in summer and grows only half the size of conventional varieties. Butterfly magnet!

Middle Layers: Southern Living's Abelia 'Miss Lemon' and Loropetalum 'Purple Daydream' both attract-bees and butterflies, and offer continuous color.

Border: 'Touch of Gold' holly from Southern Living Plants

Viburnum 'Steady Eddy'
(Proven Winners)

Loropetalum 'Purple Daydream'
(Southern Living Plants)_

Abelia 'Miss Lemon'
(Southern Living Plants)

'Touch of Gold' Holly
(Southern Living Plants)

Annuals Planted in the Pots

Planted in the pots: Alocasia in the largest pots, Heuchera 'Plum Pudding' in all pots. The colors of these leaves co-ordinate well with the shrubs planted in the ground, shown left.

I had originally planned to use white pots in this section because the colors match the white flowers of the viburnum (not shown in this photo). I realized when the pots were being installed that the white didn't stand out enough. So I tried these turquoise pots and loved them!

Coleus 'Flamethrower Salsa Verde'

Celosia 'Intenz Lipstick'

Coleus 'Pineapple Splash'

Section 3: Bright Shrubs & Perennials Planted in the Ground

There is nothing subtle about the colors featured in this section! I used neon-bright shrubs and perennials. The lime 'Touch of Gold' holly provides a unifying border.

Three Color Layers:

Tallest: Southern Living's 'It's a Breeze' rose. It's repeat bloomer, flowering in spring and fall.
Middle: 'Solar Flare' poker from the Pyromania collection. Spikey habit & grass-like foliage adds a different texture to the garden.
Shortest Layers: Proven Winners Spirea 'Double Play Candy Corn.' An amazing plant that changes color from red to orange to yellow. Plus 'Lakota Fire' Echinacea, which blooms in three colors: Red, orange, and pinkish red.
Border: 'Touch of Gold' Holly from Southern Living Plants

Spirea 'Double Play Candy Corn' (Proven Winners)

'Solar Flare' Poker Plant (Proven Winners)

'It's A Breeze' Rose (Proven Winners)

'Lakota Fire' Echinacea (Proven Winners)

'Touch of Gold' Holly (Southern Living Plants)

Bright Annuals Planted in the Pots

Basket: ZGVS16 - 16" single, side-planted basket mounted on a ZPSBK basket column kit for large pots from kinsmangarden.com.

Left: Red pots are planted with yellow shrimp plants, purple and red pentas, and lime coleus. They are underplanted with 'Surdiva Sky Blue' scaevola. See pages 68 - 71 for more info on both sets of red planters.

Right: Red pots planted with purple Persian shield, golden shrimp plants, and yellow lantana.

Section 4: Red, White & Blue Shrubs & Perennials

The red and blue colors are intensified by the white salvia and purple loropetalum. And the lime green Ilex makes the whole section pop!

Three Color Layers:

Tallest: Proven Winner's Hibiscus 'Blue Chiffon' forms the centerpiece. It features a unique, lacy center creates an anemone-like bloom.

Middle Layers: Proven Winners Rose 'Oso Easy Double Red' attracts both bees and butterflies and blooms first in spring and reblooms in fall.

Lower Layer: Salvia 'Snow Kiss' and 'Violet Profusion' from Proven Winners, butterfly magnets.

Border: 'Touch of Gold' Holly from Southern Living Plants

Pots feature a spectacular cobalt blue glaze. They are planted with a yellow canna, 'Baby Wing Red' begonias, and lantana 'Little Lucky Pot of Gold'

Once again, I wouldn't have thought that turquoise pots would work with the red, white, burgundy, and white color scheme. I tried them during the installation and just loved them! Also shown left, are 'It's a Breeze' red rose and salvia 'Violet Profusion.'

The pots are planted with these plants:

Alocasia
1 plant from a 8" pot

Persian Shield
2 plants from 4" pots
Plant Profile: Page 163

'Flamethrower Chipotle'
Coleus
6 plants from 4" pots
Plant Profile: Page 156

'Soiree Kawai Blueberry Kiss'
Vinca Hybrid
4 plants from 4" pots
Plant Profile: Page 165

This page:

I include edibles in many of my container gardens. This tomato plant is supported by a copper obelisk, which is much more attractive than a tomato cage.

'Lizard Leaf' Celosia
2 plants from 6″ pots
Plant Profile: Page 156

Opposite page:

These beautiful container gardens accent this pretty entry and say 'welcome' to visitors.

Chapter 6

My Butterfly Gardens

To learn about container gardening, I planted all the plants you see in this book and have observed them for decades. My had an office that overlooks my gardens. I spend more time looking out of the window than writing!

My trial gardens are my workshop. I learn which plants work and which don't. I particularly pay attention to how long they lived, whether they bloomed continuously, and how easy they were.

My gardens always included a lot of container gardens.

During this decades-long process, I was fascinated by watching the butterflies as much as watching the flowers. I call my butterflies 'flying flowers.' These beautiful creatures grew quite used to me and allowed me to do all my garden chores without flying away.

I had large, in-ground gardens in both my Florida house and my first Georgia house.

This chapter shows some images of my gardens. I am happy to have this opportunity to share them with you!

Left and above: Swallowtail butterflies

The Porch Garden

I designed this arbor to accommodate a seating area as well as lots of containers. It works great, holding hundreds of colorful flowers just as I wanted. The mulch floor is ideal for flowers because they can shed their little hearts out without making a mess.

The chairs and bench provide a wonderful place to sit and enjoy the flowers and butterflies.

Hanging baskets are hung from the beams, while wall pots are hung from the back wall.

Measuring only eight by ten feet, this arbor is ideal for someone who wants a lot of flowers in a small space.

The red flowers in the front are geraniums, planted next to yellow melampodium and pink cleomes. The pots feature a mass of colorful flowers and leaves, including pentas, daisies, coleus, cosmos, dragon wing begonias, petunias, variegated mint, melampodium, and double impatiens.

The Porch Garden

The plantings in my porch garden changed frequently so I could test more plants. Check out the plantings around the bench in these photos, plus the photos on the previous page. After the plants in a planter reached the end of their lifespan, I replaced them with others. This way, I learned as much as I could about the different plant species. The bowl, shown above, is detailed on pages 54 and 55.

Left: Of the six flowers clustered around the chairs in my gardens, three species (gerber daisies, lilies, and kalanchoe) bloomed for for a short time - about 2 weeks. The New Guinea impatiens and dragon wing begonias bloomed the entire growing season! I recommend taking this book with you to the garden center to check the bloom period of each plant. That fact can be hard to find online.

The Swing Garden

This garden is called the swing garden for obvious reasons! I loved sitting in the swing (from Uwharrie Chair Company) and enjoying the flowers and butterflies. Golden shrimp plants form the larger layer (growing about as tall as the swing) are great butterfly attractors, along with the red pentas and melampodium border. The sheer number of different flowers attracted hordes of butterflies.

The pots are planted with hot pink pentas and purple heliotrope. White torenia and yellow melampodium are planted in the ground. Even if you just have enough space for a few pots, the butterflies should find you!

More Swing Garden Images

I love placing side-planted border columns in butterfly gardens because it increases the number of flowers in a space. The baskets on these columns are planted with quite a variety of plants including red and purple impatiens, yellow violas, Schizanthus 'Treasure Trove Bicolor', and Lysimachia 'Outback Sunset'. White 'Odorata' begonias are planted in the ground.

The goal of spacing the columns is to keep the plants in the different baskets from touching one another when they are mature. That can be deceiving for beginners because the baskets grow so large as they mature. I started with a 30″ distance between columns, and they grew together quickly. I now use a minimum of 40″ in between the columns in a single grouping. These columns are spaced a full, five feet apart.

Butterfly Heaven

These baskets on border columns were magnets for butterflies. Quite a few of the butterfly photos you see in this book were photographed here. The butterflies spent the most time on the pink pentas and blue salvia, but sampled all the rest of the blooming plants as well. Baskets also include coleus, pink and white begonias, dusty miller, and blue, upright torenia.

These baskets are a full, 4′ apart. The border columns (black posts) measure 36″, 42″, and 48″ high. Border columns and baskets from kinsmangarden.com.

Porch Garden

Hanging baskets, window boxes, and baskets on columns - along with annual plantings in the ground -completely transformed my porch.

Side-planted window boxes are ideal for railings. These are planted with dracaena 'Lemon Lime' as centerpieces and impatiens, creeping Jenny, and coleus as side and edge plantings.

The basket on a column next to the steps is planted with a caladium centerpiece along with begonias and New Guinea impatiens along the edge and in the sides.

Look at the photo on this page. See the three hooks installed in the top beam for hanging baskets? With 70 inches in between the columns, I planned for three baskets of staggered heights. But, the side-planted baskets quickly grew together. One basket - and only a small one (16" single layer) filled that large space! I am continually surprised by how large plants grow in these containers (kinsmangarden.com)!

Entry Walk Garden

These baskets on columns 36", 42", and 48" tall. I like this size range best for groups of three columns (kinsmangarden.com). White wax begonias are planted in the ground below. The baskets are planted with New Guinea impatiens, 'Dark Star' coleus, lime coleus, torenia, creeping Jenny, and grasses.

I love this planting! And so did the butterflies, Remember, they love bright-colored flowers. The baskets are planted with begonias, mixed coleus and grasses. Salvia in mixed colors is planted in the ground.

Chapter 7

Container Plant Information

I learned about butterfly plants from observation and research. When I discovered a new plant that attracted butterflies, I tested it. I was looking for plants that were beneficial to both butterflies and gardeners. Most gardeners are looking for easy plants.

I also carefully watched all my container gardens, learning which plants attracted the most butterflies. This chapter details the best of these plants. It will also let you know which plants died quickly, or were otherwise unpleasant to grow.

Take this book with you to your garden center. Find a plant and look it up before you buy it. If it meets your expectations, plant and enjoy!

Above and left: Monarch butterflies

Plant Information

Alyssum prefers temperatures between 36 and 85 degrees. It lived about 3 months in my Florida and Georgia gardens and looks great along the edges of containers because of its unique, frothy texture. It comes in shades of white, purple, pink and red. Even though it's short lived, the lacy texture makes it worth growing. Grow it in full sun and expect it to attract a lot of butterflies.

Angelonia was a hit or miss plant until the introduction of 'Serena' angelonia, which proved to be a really high performer. It never stopped blooming for six months in my trials. Plant it when temperatures range from 45 to 100 degrees in light shade to full sun. Angelonia grows from about 13" to 16" tall and comes in white, pink, and different shades of lavender. It attracts butterflies, bees, and hummingbirds.

Begonias, dragon wing have consistently been one of the superstars in any combo I plant. They bloom all season, and I've never seen a pest or disease problem on the hundreds of plants I've tested. I use them as side or edge plants in many container gardens, where they grow about 4" to 6" tall. Place them in the center of a larger container, and they could grow as tall as 2' tall by 1' wide. They grow in any frost-free season. In tropical areas, they live as long as 2 years. Grow in medium shade to full sun. These wonderful plants come in red or pink and are frequently visited by butterflies and hummingbirds.

Begonias, wax are another one of the most dependable plants I tried. They bloom constantly in sun or shade with very little care for at least 6 months. I fertilize them at planting time and just leave them alone afterwards, except for watering. Flowers come in white, pink, or red on green or bronze leaves. They grow in medium shade to full sun and thrive in temperatures ranging from 40 to 100 degrees. They tolerate a slight frost but not a freeze. Wax begonias grow about 8" tall in the top of a container and 4" to 6" when planted in the side of a side-planted planter. Butterflies and bumblebees love the nectar from the flowers.

Blue Ribbon Plants Are Defined on Pages 34 - 35

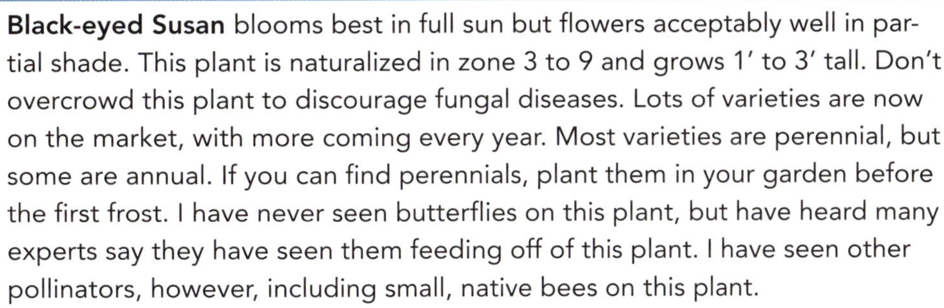

Black-eyed Susan blooms best in full sun but flowers acceptably well in partial shade. This plant is naturalized in zone 3 to 9 and grows 1′ to 3′ tall. Don't overcrowd this plant to discourage fungal diseases. Lots of varieties are now on the market, with more coming every year. Most varieties are perennial, but some are annual. If you can find perennials, plant them in your garden before the first frost. I have never seen butterflies on this plant, but have heard many experts say they have seen them feeding off of this plant. I have seen other pollinators, however, including small, native bees on this plant.

Calibrachoa - I have a love-hate relationship with this plant. It looks so gorgeous in the garden centers in spring that I always buy way more than I should. The problem with this plant is that it only lives for about 4 to 8 weeks, nowhere near as long as the blue-ribbon plants described in this book. The flowers resemble small petunias and come in every color and pattern (yes, pattern!) that you could imagine. When it dies, I replace it with blue-ribbon plants. The flowers attract hummingbirds, butterflies, and bees and grow best in full sun.

California daisy is a fabulous plant. It's both the easiest and longest-lived plant I have found that looks like a daisy. It blooms almost continuously for about 6 months with very little care. Plant in light shade to full sun when temperatures vary between 35 and 90 degrees. Although this plant grows as a perennial in tropical areas, it performs best as an annual in most areas. This cheerful plant grows about 18″ tall by 12″ wide in large containers. If it is planted very close together with other plants, it might grow to 14″ tall by 8″ wide. This wonderful plant lasts about 6 months.

Canna lilies are terrific for hot-weather plantings. They are perennials that are usually used as annuals in midsummer plantings, so they are usually found in garden centers at that time. Their only drawback is a tendency to attract pests. Different varieties grow different sizes. Look for the smaller ones of containers. Most varieties grow 3′ to 5′ tall by 2′ to 3′ wide. Dwarfs grow about 2′ tall in a container. The flowers come in pink, yellow, peach, coral, and orange. Leaves come in bronze, green, purple, or burgundy, solid or striped. I've had them last up to 2 years in containers in a frost-free area.

Plant Information

Celosia blooms all the time and lasts for up to 6 months with no care other than water if you follow the planting instructions in the first chapter. It is best used as a centerpiece. Although many reseed, mine have not. There are many varieties, some quite tall, which can reseed enough to be a nuisance. I've been lucky enough to find small varieties in local garden centers, which have never reseeded in my garden. Plant them in light shade to full sun. Celosia flowers attract butterflies and bees. They are considered a tender perennial in zones 9 and 10, or a hardy annual otherwise.

Cleome features a beautiful flower that sometimes reseeds. However, it's never happened to my cleomes. This plant can make a container garden look spectacular. I use it with pink, blue, and white flowers in full sun. Unfortunately, this plant doesn't bloom continuously, only off and on. So, plant it with enough other varieties of long-blooming annuals to keep your container garden looking good all the time. It's best to deadhead (remove spent blooms) this plant to encourage more flowers. Cleome is a summer annual, so protect it from frost. The nectar attracts butterflies and bees.

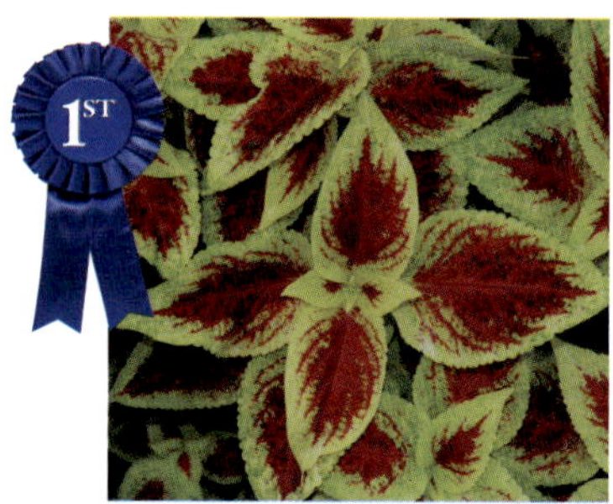

Coleus thrives planted either as a centerpiece or side plant. Just plant (following the instructions in Chapter 1) and trim occasionally to keep it tidy. Coleus tolerates temperatures down to 38 degrees. Plant it in light shade to full sun. I haven't ever had pest problems with this plant; however, I've heard of occasional problems with aphids, mites, mealybugs, slugs, and snails. This plant does quite well when planted in the side holes of side-planted baskets. There are many cultivars ranging in size from 6″ to 36″ tall. Coleus flowers attract butterflies and bees. However, I usually trim them off because they are spindly.

Coneflower is a commonly-used perennial with pretty flowers in shades of mauve, white, yellow, purple and bright pink. It is considered a star perennial in the garden when grown in light shade to full sun. I started using it in containers when I noticed dwarf varieties at the garden centers. The original coneflowers grow 2′ to 3′ tall while the newer ones grow half that size, fitting nicely when tucked into a pot. They look a lot neater if spent blooms are removed.

Blue Ribbon Plants Are Defined on Pages 34 - 35

Coreopsis is one of the 10 best-selling perennials. There are many different types, but my experience has been primarily with the threadleaf coreopsis (pictured), which differs from the rest because of its tiny, thread-like leaves. Use it as a centerpiece in an informal, wildflower-look arrangement in full sun. Blooms in most of the country from May or June through July, with another flush of flowers in fall. This plant might not look good in a nursery pot, but it looks good when planted in a larger, 16″ to 18″ container. Flowers attract bees and butterflies.

Cosmos became of the more popular pollinator plants in my containers once I figured out which size to grow. I grow this delightful plant from seed and have only tried the yellow, orange, and red ones. I planted a larger variety in the pot on page 1 of this book in a 24″ diameter pot and decided it was too big for my container gardens. I now order dwarf varieties online and plant them in pots at least 12″ wide. I They sprout and bloom quickly, living a few months. Extremely easy to grow. The bees and butterflies love it!

Creeping Jenny doesn't attract butterflies but I use it frequently in combination with butterfly-attracting plants. It trails over the sides of a container beautifully. Plus, the small leaves contrast well with plants that have larger leaves, like coleus. This vine doesn't overwhelm a planter like sweet potato vine. Plant in summer with lots of butterfly flowers and expect it to die back in the first freeze. It usually reappears in the following spring in zones 4 to 9. Use it as an annual in zones 9 and 10. Plant in medium shade to full sun.

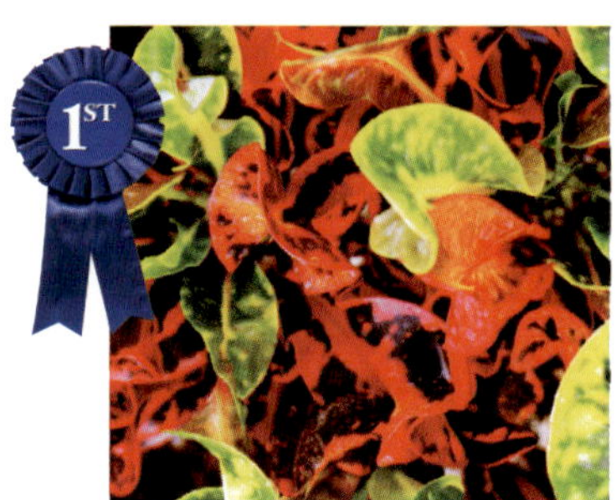

Crotons are one of the most colorful plants. Like creeping Jenny, they don't attract butterflies but add a wonderful pop of color when combined with butterfly plants in a container. Use when temperatures range from 40 to 100 degrees in medium shade to full sun. Sizes of the different cultivars vary widely, from dwarfs to small trees. Be careful with milky sap that can irritate skin and stain clothing. Plant with flowering butterfly plants in bright colors, especially red and yellow.

Plant Information

Dichondra 'Silver Falls' is another foliage plant that doesn't attract butterflies but greatly helps the appearance of a container garden. It falls smoothly like a waterfall down the side of a container. I've seen it grow 8 feet long! Plant it with butterfly-attracting plants in colors of pink, blue, and purple when temperatures vary between 45 degrees and the low-100's. Plant it in full sun to light shade. I've never had a pest problem with this plant but have heard of occasional infestations of spider mites. It lasts all spring, summer, and fall.

Dill tastes good to both people and black swallowtail butterfly caterpillars. The adult butterflies lay their eggs on this plant. Once the eggs hatch, the caterpillars devour dill. I love the texture of dill and occasionally use it in a mixed container garden. However, it's more functional to plant it by itself in a pot. That way, your whole elaborate container garden is not ruined when the caterpillars devour most of it! It grows 12" to 36" tall in a container, depending on the variety. Look for fernleaf dill, which grows more compactly and doesn't fall over, like larger cultivars will do. Grow in light shade to full sun.

Dracaena, Tricolor is one of my favorite for centerpieces in containers even though it doesn't attract butterflies. Check out the combo on pages 80 - 81. That planting attracted hordes of butterflies because the dracaena was surrounded with five other butterfly-loving plants in coordinating colors. The dracaena added texture to the arrangement. Take care with the sap of this plant because its sap is a skin irritant that is poisonous when eaten. Use in sun or shade when temperatures range from 32 to 100 degrees. I've never had a pest on this plant.

Dutchman's Pipe or Pipevine is definitely the weirdest flower in my garden. I grow it in pots about 16" in diameter with a large trellis for support. This plant is a host plant for the pipevine swallowtail butterfly. It grows huge in zones 9b to 11, sending out runners that are 15' to 20' long. I order it online for my Georgia garden (zone 7) and grow it as a summer annual. Treat it like pet food - expect to see lots of chewed leaves and flowers. But, the benefit is lots of butterflies. I've had as many as 15 flying around my pipevines at one time! Grow it ideally in light shade.

Fennel is the host plant for the eastern black swallowtail butterfly. Plant it in full sun in a pot of at least 14″ diameter. When planted alone, it may fall over and require staking. This is one of the few host plants that I have planted in mixed containers and I really like the effect of the fine texture with coarser textures. The plant grows 2′ to 3′ tall, depending on variety, if planted alone. It prefers cooler temperatures.

Gaillardia is a native, short-lived perennial that attracts butterflies and bees. It grows 24″ tall with a 20″ spread in the ground but remains much smaller in a container. New varieties are being introduced frequently, many of them smaller than the original plant. It is very tolerant of high heat and humidity, and it blooms most of the summer. Grow in full sun in zones 4 to 9. Gaillardia is highly toxic to humans. Pair them with other wildflowers, like cosmos and coreopsis.

Geraniums miss a ribbon because they require dead-heading to look good. However, it's a classic container plant that's great for pollinators. And I have neglected dead-heading a few times with no regrets. Geraniums are one of my favorite plants for centerpieces but take care to plant shorter plants around them. They prefer temperatures between 35 and 90 degrees and light shade to full sun. I've never experienced a pest on this plant, but I've heard of occasional spider mite infestations. Most geraniums grow 12″ to 14″ tall and come in many shades of red, pink, peach, white, and lavender.

Gomphrena is an excellent summer annual that adds interesting texture to the garden. It blooms for most of the growing season in full sun. The gomphrena that I have grown in containers grows about 8″ tall when planted in a container with other plants. The flowers are white, pink or purple and they provide nectar for a variety of pollinators. They also produce seeds that the birds love.

Plant Information

Helichrysum 'Icicles' is a small, filler plant that I use occasionally. It doesn't attract butterflies but adds an interesting texture and color to container gardens. I never tried it in the heat of the Georgia summer. It prefers light shade to full sun and grows about 5" tall by 5" wide in a container.

Heliotrope is not my favorite plant for container gardens in hot areas. I've seen it growing well in cooler areas, like Vancouver and parts of California. The flowers are beautiful, but the plant does not stay in bloom. It blooms for a month or so and then goes out of bloom for 2 months, blooming again for another month. All parts of the plant are toxic.

Impatiens, regular are one of the world's most popular annuals. They literally bloom their heads off from the day you plant them until the day you remove them. Since they are very thirsty plants, plant them with other plants that like tolerate daily watering in warmer temperatures, 40 - 90 degrees. Impatiens grow in shade in temperatures up to the high-90's. Take some full sun, but wilt continuously when the temperatures get into the high 80's. They grow 12" tall by equally as wide and live for about 6 months. Great plant for butterflies and bumblebees.

Impatiens, New Guinea have more color impact than most container plants. Some have colorful leaves, as shown left. They require a lot of water, but not as much as regular impatiens. I water mine everyday once the temperature get into the high 80's and they are planted in the sun. They bloom as well in shade and don't require as much water. I've never tried them in temperatures over 90 degrees in sun. They grow 8" to 12" tall and are sometimes bothered by fungus, slugs, and Japanese beatles. These showy plants are a favorite for my bumblebees and hummingbirds.

Jatropha is grown as a shrub in tropical areas. Lately, I've noticed it in garden centers with temperate climates, being sold as a summer annual. It's a great plant for seasonal use because it blooms all the time and attracts LOTS of butterflies. If you are lucky enough to see one in a garden center, buy it! Plant it in light shade to full sun. In the tropics, it grows 4' to 8' tall. It would grow that large in a huge pot but will stay much smaller as the centerpiece of a mixed flower arrangement.

Kalanchoe blossfeldiana is a really pretty plant that is in the succulent family. There are 125 species of kalanchoe and many others out-perform the blossfeldiana, which has a very short lifespan. I have found it occasionally useful when I need a short-lived, strong, color accent. It is used more indoors in a sunny window than outdoors.

Lantana is one of the best butterfly plants in this book, and it's also really easy to grow. The older, 'New Gold' cultivar blooms almost every day, while the newer cultivars sometimes take a rest in between bloom bursts. It tolerates temperatures between 32 and 95 degrees in light shade to full sun. Different varieties range from 6" to 30" tall, although most garden centers only stock the smaller ones. Colors include yellow, orange, burnt orange, white, burgundy, and lots of bi-colors.

Marigolds are an easy annual that the butterflies love. And the bees flock to it as well. However, it doesn't last as long as other, blue ribbon, yellow or orange plants including melampodium, lantana, and torenia. However, butterflies need variety, so I usually plant a few marigolds each summer. Plus, I've never seen a plant attract more bumblebees, and I spoil my bumblebees! Plant when the temperatures range between 32 degrees and the low-90's in light shade to full sun. Sizes of this plant range from 6" to 30" tall, but you'll usually find the smaller ones in your local garden centers. I've never had one last more than 2 months.

Plant Information

Melampodium, along with yellow lantana and torenia, is my favorite summer yellow flower. It blooms all summer long with very little care. However, it doesn't like temperatures below 50 degrees. Plant in medium shade to full sun. Melampodium grows to about 12" tall and lasts a full 6 months. I've never seen a pest bother this plant, and pollinators flock to it. Melampodium thrives when planted in the side holes of side-planted baskets or the top of any container.

Milkweed is the host plant for monarch butterflies. There are 30 different varieties in the US. Monarchs lay their eggs only on this plant, so it is very important to include milkweed in your butterfly gardens - if monarchs visit your location. Butterflies don't care if the plant is blooming or not because their babies (caterpillars) just eat the leaves. I always keep at least three plants on my deck because once those eggs hatch, the caterpillars will need A LOT of food. My favorite variety is *Asclepias tuberosa*, pictured. Buy it online if you can't find it at a local nursery. For more information, see page 41.

Mona lavender does very well in containers in medium shade to full sun. However, I've never been able to coax it into bloom in the heat of summer. It blooms well in temperatures ranging from 36 to 80 degrees. Butterflies like it because it has a very deep, narrow flower. They use their proboscis to get to nectar deep inside the flower. This plant grows about 16" to 18" tall with about the same spread. This plant lives for about 6 months.

Parsley is the first plant I would plant in a butterfly garden because it is the host plant for the black swallowtail butterfly (if you live in this swallowtail's range). The swallowtails will spend a lot more time in your garden if you provide host as well as nectar plants for them. Host plants for many butterflies are hard to find in garden centers, but not parsley. I have heard that the butterflies prefer curled over Italian parsley but have never tested that theory. Both parsleys grow about 12" tall by equally as wide in a container. Grow this plant in light shade to full sun.

Blue Ribbon Plants Are Defined on Pages 34 - 35

Passionflower vine is the larval host plant of the gulf fritillary and the zebra long-wing butterflies. There are about forty different passionflowers in the bottom half of the US. They grow as an annual in the rest of the country. Passionflowers require really large containers because they grow quite large. They are ideal for planting in a container on a raised deck so they can cascade over the railing and down to the ground. Or plant them in a large pot (over 16″ wide) with a sturdy support. I avoid planting them in the ground because they are hard to control, especially *Passiflora biflora*, which is considered invasive. Grow in full sun.

Pentas have it all! It's not only a star pollinator for butterflies, hummingbirds, and bees but also flowers every day for the entire growing season with very little care. Plant in light shade to full sun in any frost-free season. There are many varieties on the market, with sizes varying from 8″ to 24″ tall. Flowers are red, pink, purple, or white. Pentas will last for the entire growing season in most locations. Pentas attracted more butterflies than any other plant in my gardens.

Persian shield is a spectacular container plant. The leaves are so gorgeous they almost look artificial. It requires nothing but water for a single season's use. Plant when the temperatures range from 40 degrees to the mid-90's in medium shade to full sun. Use this plant as a centerpiece plant - it doesn't do well in the sides of side-planted baskets. In the top of a planter, it grows about 16″ tall by 8″ wide. Persian shield lives for about a year if protected from frost. I use it as a summer annual in my zone 7 garden. The flowers attract butterflies and bees, but they don't appear often.

Petunias are one of the most popular container plants in the world. However, many of the unnamed varieties are quite short lived, so they don't rate a ribbon. Expect great performance if the petunia is branded from a company you trust. Otherwise, it may be short-lived. Plant in light shade to full sun in frost-free temperatures. Watch out for fungus and whiteflies. Expect petunias to grow about 6″ tall. The trailing varieties vary in spread - up to 3′ across. Petunias come in shades of red, purple, white, yellow, and pink.

Plant Information

Phlox is a beautiful, native perennial that blooms for about 4 weeks in mid-summer and keeps blooming for another month if you deadhead it. The original phlox is too large for most containers, but dwarf varieties are now on the market. Bumble bees, honeybees, butterflies, and hummingbirds frequently visit it. Plant it in light shade to full sun in zones 3 to 8.

Plumbago is a great perennial in the ground in zones 9 to 11. It is not my favorite container plant, however, because of its sporadic bloom cycle, meaning it goes in and out of bloom during the warm season. However, it is also the host plant to cassius blue butterflies and offers the additional benefit of high heat tolerance. Plant it in full sun, and expect it to grow about 18″ tall by 14″ wide in a container.

Ruellia is not my favorite container plant because it grows long and lanky in containers - which causes it to frequently fall over. Plus, if it escapes into your yard, it can take over! Grows about 2′ tall. Light shade to full sun. It's only redeeming feature is that the pollinators drink nectar from it.

Salvia, blue is one of the easiest annuals in my containers. I plant them when the danger of frost is over and then I just add water until the first freeze in fall. They bloom profusely the entire time. The spiky flowers attract both butterflies, bees and hummingbirds. Blue salvia grows to about 18″ tall by 9″ wide in a container. I plant a few together as a centerpiece in a large pot. This is one of the most popular plants amongst the pollinators who frequent my container gardens.

Blue Ribbon Plants Are Defined on Pages 34 - 35

Salvia, red are versatile, carefree flowers that enrich the container garden with fresh colors and upright form. They are also a favorite pollinator plant for butterflies and hummingbirds. Plant them in light shade to full sun in spring or summer. Unlike the blue salvia, the red salvia requires deadheading to maintain a neat and tidy look. This plant grows about 8" tall and is extremely easy to grow.

Scaevola is an incredible annual. It blooms non-stop in temperatures from 45 degrees to the low-100's with profuse white or blue flowers. It lives for at least seven months with no care other than water! Plant when temperatures vary between 45 degrees and the low-100's in light shade to full sun. This plant trails, but not too far, and looks great either planted through the side holes or on the top of a side-planted container. I've never seen it trail more than about 12", but have heard it grows longer with less trimming. The flowers attract bees, butterflies, and other pollinating insects.

Shrimp plant is a tropical plant used as a short-term perennial in the warmest parts of the country, zones 9 - 11. It blooms continuously from spring planting time to the first frost of the fall. The spiky flower shape is also an excellent textural addition to many container arrangements. Use it as a centerpiece in light shade to full sun, although it prefers a break from noon summer sun. Use as a centerpiece, and keep a close eye out for caterpillars and snails. Butterflies and hummingbirds absolutely love them!

Snapdragons are one plant I didn't like as well in containers as I do in the ground because they went out of bloom on me. The tall ones are gorgeous in containers, however, and tolerate a light frost but not freezing weather. Grow when temperatures vary between 32 degrees and the low-80's in light shade to full sun. Sizes vary between 6" and 36" tall. Expect only a 2 - 3 month lifespan for this gorgeous annual. Bumblebees are the primary pollinator of snapdragons because they have the ability to open the tight flowers for easy access. Butterflies follow, once the flowers are open and accessible.

Plant Information

Sweet potato vines are usually used for their leaf color, which ranges from lime green to purple to variegated white-pink-green. However, they sometimes flower and the blooms are quite attractive to butterflies. I seldom see either flowers or butterflies on mine, so I grow them for the leaf color. Look for the 'Sweet Caroline' variety - which is more compact than many others. Plant these in medium shade to full sun. Look out for lots of pests, including snails (lots of them), fungus, white flies, and aphids.

Torenia, trailing are one of the top performers from our container trials, growing for an entire year in frost-free areas. They are very easy to grow, blooming all year in frost-free areas, even in the hottest parts of summer. Plant in any frost-free season in light shade to full sun. Torenia tolerates light frosts but not freezes and come in shades of purple, blue, red, and yellow. Expect it to grow about 6" to 12" down the sides of a planter. Torenia is a pollinator star, attracting bees, butterflies, and hummingbirds. Bumble bees will bury themselves in the throat of this flower!

Torenia, upright didn't last anywhere near as long as trailing torenia in our trials. However, it was extremely easy to grow and looked fabulous for their short lifespan. There may be newer varieties that are longer-lasting. Look for upright torenia from brands you trust. Plant when temperatures vary between 50 degrees and the low-100's in light shade to full sun. It grows about 8" tall and equally as wide and comes in blue, pink, white, red, and multi. All varieties have yellow centers. Torenia is a pollinator star, attracting bees, butterflies, and hummingbirds. Bumblebees will bury themselves in the throat of this flower!

Verbena, upright died quickly in the sides of my side-planted containers. Trailing verbena did much better, but didn't bloom consistently or last through an entire, 6-month growing season. It prefers sun and warm temperatures. Although most verbenas are annuals, the 'Homestead Purple' variety is a perennial in zones 6 to 9. It is a much better performer than the annual varieties, blooming on and off in spring, summer, and fall. Nectar from the flowers attracts butterflies, hummingbirds, and other pollinators.

Blue Ribbon Plants Are Defined on Pages 34 - 35

Vinca is a heat-tolerant annual that is extremely easy to grow. If rainfall exceeds 60" per year, they suffer. Vinca do well in containers but it doesn't bloom as much when planted in the sides of side-planted planters. Plant them in mid-June and enjoy them until the first frost. They grow about 9" tall by 7" wide in a container. Vinca flowers come in a variety of colors, including white, red, purple, and pink. They attract butterflies, bees, and hummingbirds.

Violas are similar to pansies except the flowers are smaller. They do well during the cool times of the year and thrive in shade. Plant when temperatures vary between 22 degrees and the low-80's in medium shade to full sun. They tolerate full sun in cool temperatures. Use as a mounding plant that works well in the center or along the edges of any pot as well as in the sides of hanging baskets. This small plant grows only 4" to 6" tall and equally as wide. They supply early spring pollinators with much-needed nectar.

.

Yarrow is a perennial that blooms from late May until the end of July in zones 3 to 8. Or, grow it as an annual in summer containers. If you deadhead (remove the spent blooms), it blooms a month or so longer. Yarrow flowers are either white, pink, red, yellow, orange, or lilac. The original cultivar grows a little tall in containers, reaching a height of 18" to 30" and equally as wide. However, smaller varieties are now on the market, like 'Little Moonshine,' which are perfectly-sized for containers. Yarrow attracts bees, butterflies, and other pollinators. It prefers full sun.

Zinnia is an old-time favorite of many gardeners. The tall, older varieties don't last all season because of disease. However, I buy them frequently because the flowers are so pretty, both to me and the butterflies, bees, and hummingbirds that frequent them. The 'Profusion' variety (pictured) lasts much longer because of its disease resistance. Many new hybrids have incredible flowers. I grew 12 different, cool new varieties from seed one year and just loved them. Sizes vary greatly depending on cultivar.

Index